SELECTED
PIANO COMPOSITIONS

César Franck

SELECTED PIANO COMPOSITIONS

Edited by Vincent d'Indy

Dover Publications, Inc., New York

Published in Canada by General Publishing Company, Ltd.,
30 Lesmill Road, Don Mills, Toronto, Ontario.
Published in the United Kingdom by Constable and Company,
Ltd.

This Dover edition, first published in 1976, is an unabridged
republication of the work originally published with the title
Piano Compositions by César Franck by the Oliver Ditson Company, Boston, in 1922 in the series "The Musicians Library."
The present edition is published by special arrangement with
the Theodore Presser Company, Bryn Mawr, Pennsylvania.

International Standard Book Number: 0-486-23269-7
Library of Congress Catalog Card Number: 75-27672

Manufactured in the United States of America
Dover Publications, Inc.
180 Varick Street
New York, N.Y. 10014

CONTENTS

COMPLETE LIST OF PIANO COMPOSITIONS
BY CÉSAR FRANCK

Trois esquisses (*premières compositions*)	1836
Eglogue (*Hirtengedicht*). Op. 3	} 1842
Duo sur le " God save the King," à 4 *mains*. Op. 4	
Grand caprice. Op. 5	} 1843
Souvenir d'Aix-la-Chapelle. Op. 7	
Transcription de quatre mélodies de Schubert. Op. 8	
Ballade. Op. 9	
Pièce, avec accompagnement de quintette à cordes (?). Op. 10	
Première fantaisie sur Gulistan. Op. 11	} 1844
Deuxième fantaisie sur Gulistan. Op. 12	
Fantaisie pour piano (?). Op. 13[1]	
Fantaisie sur deux airs polonais. Op. 15	} 1845
Trois petits riens (*Duettino, Valse, le Songe*). Op. 16	
Duo sur Lucile, à 4 *mains*. Op. 17	1846
Les plaintes d'une poupée	1865
Les Eolides, transcription à 4 *mains*	1875
Le Chasseur maudit, transcription à 4 *mains*	1883
Les Djinns, transcription pour *deux pianos*, à 4 *mains*	1884
Danse lente	1885
Variations symphoniques, transcription pour *deux pianos*, à 4 *mains*	1885
Prélude, Choral et Fugue	1884–85
Prélude, Aria et Final	1885–86
Symphonie en ré mineur, transcription à 4 *mains*	1888–89

[1] *Although they appear under these numbers in the catalogue of seventeen early works prepared by Franck himself, there is no information obtainable concerning the pieces listed as Op. 10 and Op. 13. Probably they were not engraved, and the manuscripts are lost or mislaid. It is even possible that the Fantaisie listed as Op. 13 in this catalogue was never composed, or that it was used over again in the writing of the Fantaisie, Op. 15.*

CÉSAR AUGUSTE FRANCK
AND HIS COMPOSITIONS FOR PIANO
1822-1890

AT the very period when the giant of the symphony, Ludwig van Beethoven, was completing the manuscript of that one among his works which he himself considered the most perfect, — I speak of the sublime *Messe Solennelle* in D major, — on the tenth of December, 1822, there was born at Liège the one who was destined to become in the symphonic succession, as well as in the realm of religious music, the true descendant of the Master of Bonn.

It was in the country of the Walloons that César Franck was born — in that country, so akin to France not only in heart and language, but even in external appearance. For what is more similar to the French central plateau than those valleys broken by abrupt and picturesque plains, where in the spring the golden broom spreads out to an almost unlimited horizon; or those low rounded hills, where the French traveller finds again with surprise the beeches and pines which are native to his cold Cévennes Mountains? It was such a country, Gallic in aspect, German in customs and surroundings, which was destined by fate to cradle the genius who should create a symphonic art that was French in spirit, clarity and form; but firmly grounded, on the other hand, upon the noble Beethovenian tradition and nourished still further by the great inheritance of classic art.

From his earliest years the mind of César Franck was turned toward music. His father, a man of stern decision, had resolved that his two sons should become musicians, and they could not do other than bow to his will. Fortunately, the outcome of this premature determination was not that which is so generally the case; for too often it leads the child to an increasing dislike, if not to actual hatred, of the career under-

AL'Epoque précise où le géant de la symphonie, Ludwig van Beethoven, venait de terminer le manuscrit de celle de ses œuvres qu'il tenait lui-même comme la plus parfaite, je veux parler de la sublime *Messe solennelle* en *ré majeur,* le 10 décembre 1822, naissait à Liège celui qui était appelé à devenir dans l'ordre symphonique aussi bien que dans l'art religieux, le véritable continuateur du maître de Bonn.

Ce fut dans le pays wallon que naquit César Franck, dans ce pays, si français non seulement de cœur et de langage, mais même d'aspect extérieur; car, quoi de plus semblable à notre plateau central de la France que ces vallées accidentées aux plans abrupts et pittoresques, que ces landes où le genêt s'épanouit au printemps en un horizon d'or quasi illimité, que ces collines, peu élevées cependant, où le voyageur français surpris retrouve les hêtres et les pins, végétation des froides montagnes cévenoles? C'était bien, en effet, ce pays, gaulois d'aspect, germain d'habitudes et de voisinage qui devait fatalement enfanter le génie prédestiné à la création d'un art symphonique bien français par son esprit de précision et de mesure, mais solidement appuyé, d'autre part, sur la haute tradition beethovénienne, résultante magnifiée des antérieures traditions de l'art musical.

Dès le plus jeune âge, l'esprit de César Franck fut tourné vers la musique. Son père, homme dur et autoritaire, avait décidé que ses deux fils seraient musiciens, ceux-ci n'avaient qu'à s'incliner devant sa décision; par bonheur, et contrairement à la plupart de ces affectations prématurées qui laissent trop souvent chez l'enfant grandissant le dégoût, parfois même la haine du métier entrepris à contre-cœur, la semence musicale tomba chez César Franck dans un terrain admirablement apte à la faire germer et fructifier.

taken without considering his preferences. With César Franck the musical seed fell upon a soil well adapted to make it grow and bear fruit.

At the age of twelve he had completed his early studies at the music school of his native town, and his father, desirous of seeing him succeed in a larger field, left home with his two sons in 1835, and established himself in Paris. There César commenced and made considerable progress in the study of counterpoint, fugue and composition with Reicha, who gave him private lessons. The following year, however, Reicha died, and the father of the future composer of *Les Béatitudes* sought admission to the Paris Conservatoire for his son; but nevertheless it was not until 1837 that the boy was received as a pupil in the class of Laborne for composition, and in that of Zimmermann for piano.

After his initial year of study he received a First Prize in fugue; and in his piano work he had the unusual experience of being placed *hors concours* in the examinations held at the end of the year 1838. This happened as follows: After he had performed with distinction the Concerto in A minor by Hummel, the test-piece appointed, what did young Franck take it into his head to do during sight-reading examination but to transpose the given piece down a third, and to play it without hesitation or error! This was an entirely irregular and unexpected proceeding, and such hardihood on the part of a pupil midway between fifteen and sixteen years old seemed almost irreverent to the old Cherubini, who refused absolutely to award the First Prize to the young contestant; but as the composer of *Lodoïska*, despite his conventional and autocratic disposition, was far from unjust, he suggested that the jury should accord to the bold pianist a special award *hors concours*, which should be designated *Grand Prix d'honneur*. It is the only time, I believe, that such an award has been made in an instrumental examination at the Conservatoire de Paris.

Having entered Berton's class in 1839, Franck received a Second Prize in that year, and the year following he won the First Prize for fugue.

In 1841 there was another surprise for the

A douze ans, il avait terminé ses premières études à l'école de musique de sa ville natale et son père, désireux de le voir réussir sur un plus vaste théâtre, émigra avec ses deux fils en 1835 et vint s'installer à Paris. Là, César commença et poussa même assez loin l'étude du contrepoint, de la fugue et de la composition avec Reicha, qui lui donnait des leçons particulières, mais celui-ci étant mort l'année suivante, le père du futur auteur des *Béatitudes* sollicita pour son fils l'admission au Conservatoire; ce ne fut toutefois qu'en 1837 que César put entrer comme élève dans la classe de Leborne pour la composition et dans celle de Zimmermann pour le piano.

Dès la première année d'études, il remportait un premier accessit de fugue; quant au piano, il lui arrivait la singulière aventure d'être classé *hors concours* aux épreuves de fin d'année de 1838, voici dans quelles circonstances. Après qu'il eut exécuté de façon tout à fait supérieure le concerto en *la mineur* de Hummel, morceau imposé, le jeune Franck ne s'avisa-t-il pas, lors de l'épreuve de *lecture à vue*, de transposer le morceau à déchiffrer à la tierce inférieure et de le jouer ainsi sans une faute ni une hésitation? Ceci n'était point prévu au règlement des concours et cette hardiesse, de la part d'un élève de quinze ans et demi, parut tellement irrévérencieuse au vieux Chérubini qu'il se refusa absolument à attribuer le premier prix au jeune concurrent, mais, comme, en dépit de son esprit formaliste et autocratique, l'auteur de *Lodoïska* n'était point injuste, il proposa au jury de décerner au pianiste téméraire une récompense spéciale hors concours que l'on dénomma: *Grand prix d'honneur.* — C'est, je le crois bien, la seule fois qu'il ait été donné, à un concours instrumental du Conservatoire de Paris, une récompense de cette nature.

Entré, en 1839, dans la classe de Berton, le jeune homme remporte, cette même année un second prix et l'année suivante, le premier prix de fugue.

En 1841, autre surprise pour le jury. César, élève de la classe de Benoist (auquel il succéda en 1872), concourait pour le prix d'orgue; ayant observé, avec son merveilleux instinct du contre-

jury. Young Franck, now a pupil of Benoist (whom he succeeded in 1872), competed for the organ prize; and having observed with his marvellous instinct for counterpoint, that the given subject for the fugue lent itself to use in combination with the theme given at the same time for improvising a sonata, he undertook to treat them simultaneously in such a way that the one served as contrast to the other. He tells us himself that he was "very happy in the combining of the two subjects;" but the thematic development which arose from this unwonted method of treating an improvisation assumed such unusual proportions that the members of the jury (Cherubini, on account of illness, was not one of them) comprehended naught of this *tour de force* so foreign to the routine at the Conservatoire, and awarded no prize at all to the troublesome boy. It happened, however, that Benoist, the instructor of the too resourceful young musician, undertook to explain the situation so that, modifying their former decision, the gentlemen of the jury decided to confer on young Franck — a Second Prize for organ!

It was perhaps from that hour that Franck became a suspect in the eyes of musical officialdom.

In 1842 (April 22) there came an order from his father, which forced César to leave the Conservatoire: he was instructed to take up the career of a "virtuoso."

It is during this period that most of his compositions for piano alone originated — arrangements for four hands, brilliant transcriptions, fantasias on themes of Dalayrue, and upon two Polish melodies — all such productions as formed the luggage then customary of the "composer-pianist."

But in spite of this forced labor, to which Franck was condemned by paternal authority with the practical aim of replenishing the family coffers, he could not restrain himself — genuine artist that he was — from searching for and finding, even in his most insignificant productions, novel patterns which, though not in any way the aesthetic forms of serious composition, did in-

point, que le sujet donné de la fugue se prêtait à des combinaisons avec le thème, également donné, de la sonate à improviser, il entreprit de les traiter simultanément de façon que l'un servit de repoussoir à l'autre. Il fut, nous racontait-il lui-même, "très heureux dans l'association de ces deux sujets," mais les développements fournis par cette manière insolite de traiter l'improvisation, prenant des proportions inusitées, les membres du jury (duquel Chérubini malade ne faisait point partie), ne comprenant rien à ce tour de force tout à fait en dehors des habitudes du Conservatoire, n'attribuèrent aucune récompense à ce gêneur. . . . Il fallut donc que Benoist, le professeur du trop ingénieux élève, vint leur expliquer la situation pour que, revenant sur leur première décision, ces MM. du jury se décidassent à accorder au jeune homme — un *second prix* d'orgue!

Dès ce moment, peut-être, Franck devint suspect aux yeux des gens officiels. . . .

Le 22 avril 1842, un ordre de son père l'obligea à quitter définitivement le Conservatoire: il lui était enjoint d'entreprendre la carrière de "virtuose."

C'est à cette époque que remontent la plupart des œuvres de piano seul, arrangements à quatre mains, transcriptions brillantes, fantaisies sur des thèmes de Dalayrue et sur deux airs polonais, tout ce qui constituait alors le bagage du *pianiste compositeur*.

Mais, malgré ces *travaux forcés* auxquels Franck était condamné de par l'autorité paternelle, dans le but pratique d'alimenter la caisse de la famille, il ne pouvait s'empêcher, en artiste sincère qu'il était, de chercher et de trouver, même dans ses plus insignifiantes productions, des *formes* nouvelles, non point encore des formes esthétiques de haute composition, mais des combinaisons de doigtés nouveaux, des dessins encore inemployés, des dispositions harmoniques donnant au piano une sonorité non encore entendue; c'est ainsi que, sans les comparer aux monuments de sa dernière manière, certaines des premières œuvres de piano du maître offrent un intérêt spécial dont l'étude peut tenter des musi-

volve new uses of the fingers, formulated designs hitherto unemployed, and distributed the harmonies so as to give to the piano a sonority never before heard. Thus it may be said, without comparing them to the works of his later manner, that certain of his early piano compositions possess a unique interest which may tempt musicians, and especially pianists, to study them. For instance, I may mention the *Eglogue*, Op. 3, and the *Ballade*, Op. 9, without including the trios for piano, violin and violoncello, Op. 1 and Op. 2, which deserve particular mention.

Franck composed these first three trios while still a student at the Paris Conservatoire, and his father had directed that he should dedicate them to H.M. Leopold I, King of Belgium. If I remember rightly a conversation which I once had with Franck upon this matter, it followed directly upon an audience at Court, after young César had presented his works to his august patron, that he was forced by paternal authority suddenly to leave the Conservatoire, as his father based fantastic hopes upon this dedication. Unfortunately, nothing to justify them came to pass in spite of a sojourn of nearly two months in Belgium.

However that might be, the first trio in F♯ marks a step in the history of music; for it really is the first composition which, following the principle indicated by Beethoven in his last quartets, establishes frankly—one might almost say naïvely—the great cyclic form, which no other composer since the Ninth Symphony had either recognized or dared to use.

We have no further details concerning the stay in Belgium, except that Franck met Liszt there, and from this meeting was born the fourth trio. It is probable, however, that his father reaped none of the benefits which he hoped to find there; for in 1844 we find the entire family established again in Paris, with no other resources than the lessons or concerts which were given by the two sons, Joseph and César.

This was the opportune moment which the latter chose in which to marry.

Having been in love for some time with a

ciens et surtout des pianistes; je citerai comme exemple l'*Eglogue*, op. *3* et la *Ballade*, op. *9*, sans compter les trios pour piano, violon et violoncelle, op. *1* et *2*, qui méritent une mention particulière.

Franck écrivit ses trois premiers trios alors qu'il était encore au Conservatoire de Paris, son père lui en dicta la dédicace: *à S. M. Léopold 1ᵉʳ, roi des Belges*, et, si je me souviens bien d'une entretien que j'eus avec mon maître à ce sujet, il en résulterait que ce fut précisément à l'occasion d'une audience de cour où le jeune César devait présenter ses œuvres à leur auguste dédicataire, qu'il dut subitement abandonner le Conservatoire, son père fondant sur la dédicace en question les plus fantastiques espérances que rien, hélas, ne vint justifier dans la suite, malgré un séjour de près de deux ans en Belgique.

Quoiqu'il en soit, le premier trio en *fa dièse* marque une étape dans l'histoire de l'art. Cette œuvre, en effet, est la première en date qui, partant du principe posé par Beethoven en ses derniers quatuors, établisse franchement, on pourrait dire naïvement, la grande *forme cyclique* que nul musicien, depuis l'auteur de la IXᵉ Symphonie, n'avait su ou osé employer.

On ne possède aucun détail sur le séjour que fit le maître en Belgique sinon qu'il y rencontra Liszt et que, de cette rencontre naquit le quatrième trio, mais il est probable que le père n'en tira point les avantages qu'il y était allé chercher, puisque, dès 1844, nous retrouvons toute la famille installée de nouveau à Paris et sans beaucoup d'autres ressources que les cachets, leçons ou concerts, que pouvaient fournir à la communauté les deux fils, Joseph et César.

Ce fut le moment que celui-ci choisit pour se marier.

Epris, depuis quelques temps déjà d'une jeune artiste dramatique, fille d'une tragédienne alors célèbre, Madame Desmousseaux, il l'épousa, malgré les récriminations de ses parents effrayés de voir une *femme de théâtre* entrer dans leur famille.

Et alors, commença pour le maître cette vie de labeur incessant et régulier qui se déroula sans trêve et sans à-coups pendant un demi-

young actress, the daughter of a celebrated trage-
dienne, Madame Desmousseaux, he made her his
wife in spite of the protests of both his parents,
who were scandalized to see a young woman of
the theatre brought into the family.

Now there began for Franck that life of regular and unremitting toil which lasted without
a break for fifty years, and which allowed him
no diversion except (and that but seldom) a concert where one of his works was given.

It was the first performance of his *Ruth*, a
Biblical pastoral in three parts, which took place
on January 4, 1846, in the Salle of the Conservatoire, that brought Franck a certain success,
though without further result. Most of the professional critics saw in the work merely a "banal
imitation" of *Le Désert* by Félicien David, which
was then in the enjoyment of a vigorous, though
ephemeral, success. A little later it was the name
of Richard Wagner that the musical scribes em-
ployed, with which to crush every new work;
and that habit is still in force to-day, when the
same scribes are ready to exalt *a priori* every
youthful production, whatever its worth, at the
expense of the masterpieces of an earlier day —
a curious reversal of procedure.

However, one of the critics in 1846, with
better judgment than his fellows, wrote of *Ruth*
as follows: "M. Franck is naïve, exceedingly
so; and this simplicity has, we believe, served
him well in the composition of his Biblical oratorio." Twenty-five years later, September 24,
1871, there took place at the Cirque d'été, under
the composer's own direction, a second performance of *Ruth*; and the same critic, perhaps without remembering that he had already heard this
oratorio, waxed enthusiastic, and wrote again:
"It is a revelation! This score, which by its charm
and melodic simplicity reminds one of Méhul's
Joseph, but with a tenderer grace and a more
modern style, may boldly be called a masterwork."

In 1851 the future composer of *Hulda* adven-
tured for the first time into dramatic music with
the *Valet de Ferme*, a rather colorless score which
furthermore was never performed. Also, after

siècle, lui apportant seulement parfois — mais
rarement — la diversion d'un concert où l'on
exécutait quelqu'une de ses œuvres.

Ce fut d'abord, le 4 janvier 1846, dans la
salle du Conservatoire, la première exécution
de *Ruth*, églogue biblique en trois parties, qui
obtint un certain succès, mais sans lendemain.
La plupart des critiques professionnels n'y
virent qu'une "plate imitation" du *Désert* de
Félicien David, dont l'éphémère renommée était
alors dans toute sa vigueur; un peu plus tard,
ce sera de Richard Wagner dont se serviront
les écrivains musicaux pour accabler tout ou-
vrage nouveau, et cette tendance durera jusqu'à
l'époque contemporaine où les mêmes écrivains
musicaux se sont pris à exalter, *a priori*, toutes
les œuvres des jeunes, de quelque valeur qu'elles
soient, au détriment des chefs-d'œuvre de l'art
ancien . . . curieux retour des choses.

Cependant, l'un des critiques de 1846, plus
avisé que les autres, écrivait ceci, à propos de
Ruth: "M. Franck est naïf, excessivement naïf,
et cette simplicité l'a, avouons-le, assez bien
servi dans la composition de son oratorio biblique." — Vingt-cinq ans plus tard, le 24 sep-
tembre 1871, eut lieu, au Cirque d'été, et sous
la direction du maître lui-même, une seconde
audition de *Ruth*, et le même critique, enthou-
siasmé, écrit cette fois, sans peut-être se rap-
peler qu'il avait déjà entendu le susdit oratorio:
"C'est une révélation! Cette partition, qui, par
le charme et la simplicité mélodique, rappelle le
Joseph de Méhul, avec une grâce plus tendre et
plus moderne, peut être hardiment qualifié de
chef-d'œuvre. . . . "

En 1851, pour la première fois, le futur compositeur d'*Hulda* abordait le genre dramatique
avec le *Valet de ferme*, partition assez incolore
qui ne fut, du reste, jamais représentée; enfin,
après avoir été, pendant quelques années, organiste de la petite paroisse Saint Jean Saint François, au Marais, Franck rencontra le calme et
pur asile qui fut le véritable berceau d'où sortit
une nouvelle manière d'être de son talent.

L'actuelle basilique de Sainte Clotilde venait
d'être achevée, remplaçant la petite église de

having been for several years organist of the little parish at Marais, Saint Jean Saint François, Franck found the calm and quiet retreat which was to be a veritable cradle in which to foster the new spirit of his genius.

The present basilica of Sainte Clotilde was nearing completion to replace the little church of Sainte Valère; and Cavaille-Coll, that master inventor who died poor, had installed there an organ of splendid sonority to which he who won the Second Prize in 1841, then organist of Sainte Valère, naturally succeeded in 1859.

It was in the twilight of that gallery at Sainte Clotilde, which I cannot recall without emotion, that the greater part of Franck's life was passed; it was there that for thirty years, every Sunday, every fête-day, every Friday morning, he fanned the flame of his genius in admirable improvisations, often higher in thought than many a piece of music chiselled with finished art. It was there, undoubtedly, that he conceived his sublime *Béatitudes*.

And so for several years he meditated, living the tranquil existence of organist and teacher; and to the feverish production of his youthful years there succeeded a period of calm during which he wrote nothing but organ pieces and religious music. This calm was but the precursor of still a third change, a final one, to which the world of music is indebted for works of the greatest value.

In 1869 a friend of the family, Madame Colomb, offered Franck the text of an oratorio following closely step by step the Gospel text of the Sermon on the Mount. He was at once fired with enthusiasm for the subject, which appealed so strongly to his devout soul and to his passionate and generous nature, and he composed the first part immediately.

His work was interrupted by an event that left no Frenchman unstirred, and Franck, though born in Belgium, was French in heart and sympathy. I refer to the Franco-Prussian War of 1870.

Though too old for active service, Franck enrolled, like every one else, in the Garde Nation-

Sainte Valère, et Cavaillé-Coll, cet inventeur de génie qui mourut pauvre, y avait construit un orgue d'une splendide sonorité dont l'ancien second prix de 1841, alors organiste de Sainte Valère prit naturellement possession en 1859.

C'est dans la pénombre de cette tribune de Sainte Clotilde dont je ne puis me souvenir sans émotion, que s'écoula la meilleure partie de sa vie; ce fut là que, chaque dimanche, chaque jour de fête, chaque vendredi matin, pendant trente ans, il vint attiser le feu de son génie en d'admirables improvisations, souvent bien plus hautes de pensée que nombre de morceaux de musique ciselés avec art; ce fut là, incontestablement, qu'il prévit ses sublimes *Béatitudes*.

Ainsi, durant près de dix ans, il se recueille, vivant sa vie tranquille d'organiste et de professeur et faisant succéder à la fièvre de production des jeunes années une période de calme où il n'écrit plus que des pièces d'orgue et de la musique religieuse; mais ce calme n'est que le précurseur d'une troisième transformation, définitive, celle-là, à laquelle l'art musical devra de hauts chefs-d'œuvre.

En l'année 1869, une amie de sa famille, Mme Colomb, lui offrit un poème d'oratorio suivant pas à pas l'évangile du *Sermon sur la montagne*. Franck s'enthousiasma pour ce sujet qui convenait si bien à son esprit croyant et à son tempérament généreux et passionné, il en écrivit aussitôt la première partie.

Ce travail fut interrompu par un événement qui ne pouvait laisser indifférente aucune âme française (et Franck, belge de naissance, était bien français de cœur et de dilection); cet événement, c'était la guerre de 1870.

Trop âgé pour prendre du service actif, Franck, enrôlé comme tout le monde dans la Garde nationale sédentaire, avait vu ses jeunes disciples se disperser au vent mauvais de nos défaites et laisser le contrepoint, l'orgue ou le piano pour aller manier le fusil dans les vaillantes armées improvisées que notre pays sut, six mois durant, opposer aux envahisseurs victorieux.

Plusieurs de ces disciples ne devaient plus revoir le maître aimé. . . . Trois d'entr'eux, Henri

ale Sédentaire, and had to see his young pupils scattered by the evil wind of defeat, leaving their study of counterpoint, organ or piano to go forth and handle the guns in the brave, hastily improvised armies, with which for six months our country endeavored to oppose the victorious invaders.

Many of his disciples never were to see again their beloved master. Three of them, Henri Duparc, Arthur Coquard and the writer of these lines (who had never yet dared to show him any of his crude efforts), were shut up with César Franck in besieged Paris. One evening, in an interval of standing guard at the outpost, Franck, brimming with enthusiasm, read to these young men an article in the *Figaro*, which extolled in a prose sufficiently poetic the superb vigor with which Paris, though sore wounded, still resisted. "I wish to set that to music," he cried, after he finished reading. A few days later, he sang to us with fervor the result of his labors, thrilling with patriotic inspiration and juvenile ardor:

"*Je suis Paris, la reine des cités,*" etc.

Never to this day has the ode been printed; but it is, I believe, the first instance of a composer venturing to set a prose poem to music.

In 1872 there came to Franck a curious and unexpected preferment—he was appointed professor of organ at the Conservatoire, no one knows how; and he, such a stranger to intrigue, understood it least of all. Old Benoist, having reached the age limit (he had taught organ since 1822), finally retired to a well-earned rest. How did it happen that a Minister of Fine Arts, by chance endowed with some vision, bethought himself of appointing to the position the organist of Sainte Clotilde who was by nature and inclination so little of a politician? It is a mystery which no one has ever solved!

But, however it befell, Franck entered upon his duties February 1, 1872, and from that very moment he was the object of animosity, whether conscious or not, from all his colleagues, who never came to regard as one of themselves an artist who placed his art above every other con-

Dupare, Arthur Coquard et celui qui écrit ces lignes (qui n'avait cependant point encore osé lui présenter ses informes essais), étaient, comme César Franck, enfermés dans Paris assiégé. Un soir, dans l'intervalle de deux gardes aux avant-postes, le maître, frémissant d'enthousiasme, lut à ces jeunes gens un article du journal le *Figaro*, dans lequel, en une prose suffisament poëtique, était célébrée la mâle fierté de ce Paris blessé, mais résistant encore: "Je veux en faire la musique!", s'écria-t-il après la lecture. Peu de jours après, il nous chantait fiévreusement le résultat de son travail, vibrant de patriotique inspiration et de chaleur juvénile:

Je suis Paris, la reine des cités, etc.

Cette ode n'a jamais été gravée jusqu'ici; c'est, je le crois, la première fois qu'un musicien osa s'aventurer à composer sur un poëme *en prose*.

En 1872, se produisit dans la carrière du maître un bien singulier accident, il fut nommé, on ne sait comment (et lui-même, si étranger à toute intrigue, le sut moins que personne), professeur d'orgue au Conservatoire. Le vieux Benoist, atteint par la limite d'âge (il enseignait l'orgue depuis 1822), prenait définitivement une retraite bien gagnée; comment se fit-il qu'un ministre des beaux-arts, par hasard clairvoyant, s'avisa de penser pour ce poste à l'organiste de Sainte Clotilde qui était si peu officiel, d'allure et d'esprit? C'est un mystère qui n'a point été élucidé.

Quoiqu'il en soit, Franck entrait en fonctions le 1er février 1872, et, dès ce moment, il fut en butte à l'animosité, consciente ou non, de ses collègues qui se refusèrent toujours à regarder comme *des leurs* un artiste plaçant l'Art au dessus de tout autre considération, un musicien aimant la Musique d'un ardent et noble amour.

Cette même année, il écrivait la première version musicale de *Rédemption*, oratorio en deux parties sur un texte, assez médiocre, d'Edouard Blau, et Colonne, alors à ses débuts comme chef d'orchestre, en dirigeait la première exécution au concert spirituel du Jeudi saint 1873.

Il s'en fallut de quelquechose que cette exécution fut satisfaisante, car M. Massenet, dont

sideration, a musician who loved music with an ardent and noble passion.

That same year he wrote the first musical setting to *Le Rédemption*, an oratorio in two parts, composed to a rather mediocre text by Edouard Blau; and Colonne, then at the beginning of his career as orchestral conductor, directed the first performance at a sacred concert on Holy Thursday, 1873. That performance, owing to certain circumstances, was far from satisfactory; for M. Massenet, whose *Marie-Magdeleine* was to be given for the first time two days later by the same performers, monopolized most of the rehearsals allotted for the two concerts, and the good Franck, without bitterness or rancor, had to content himself (and being so far from exacting, he actually *was* content) with a half reading, and a perfunctory performance, which failed to produce any effect. Owing to lack of time for preparation, he was even obliged to omit the great symphonic piece which separates the two parts of the work, and which, as a matter of fact, he completely rewrote later.

Aside from *Les Eolides*, a symphonic poem for orchestra after the verses by Leconte de Lisle, which was produced at a Concert Lamoureux in 1876 and was not in the least understood by the public, Franck worked scarcely at all during the six years following the composition of *Le Rédemption* except upon his oratorio, *Les Béatitudes*, which he did not finish until 1879, and which therefore occupied him during ten years of his life.

Convinced that he had produced a beautiful work, the master, whose innocence of mind made him an easy prey to delusions, imagined that the Government of his adopted country could not fail to be interested in the production of so noble a work, and that if the Minister could but hear his new score, he would undoubtedly appreciate it and favor a performance.

Franck therefore arranged for a private audition of *Les Béatitudes* at his modest apartment in the Boulevard Saint Michel, after having carefully ascertained what day would be convenient for the Minister of Fine Arts, and after having

le même personnel devait interpréter le lendemain pour la première fois la *Marie-Magdeleine*, absorba la presque totalité des répétitions affectées aux deux concerts, en sorte que le bon Franck, sans fiel et sans défiance, dut se contenter (et il s'en contenta, tellement il était peu exigeant), d'une quasi lecture et d'une exécution excessivement sommaire qui ne produisit aucun effet; il fut même obligé, faute de temps pour le travailler, de supprimer le grand morceau symphonique qui séparait les deux parties de son œuvre et qu'il récrivit, du reste, complètement depuis.

A part les *Eolides*, poëme pour orchestre, d'après des vers de Leconte de Lisle, qui fit une apparition au Concert Lamoureux en 1876 et ne fut nullement compris par le public, Franck ne travailla guère pendant les six années qui suivirent la composition de *Rédemption*, qu'à son oratorio les *Béatitudes* qu'il termina seulement en 1879 et qui lui prit conséquemment dix ans de sa vie.

Conscient d'avoir produit une belle œuvre, le maître, dont l'âme naïve fut constamment en proie aux illusions, s'imagina que le gouvernement de son pays d'adoption ne pouvait manquer de s'intéresser à la présentation d'une aussi haute manifestation d'art et que si le ministre connaissait sa nouvelle œuvre, il l'apprécierait sûrement et en favoriserait l'exécution.

Il organisa donc chez lui, dans son modeste rez-de-chaussée du boulevard Saint Michel, une audition privée des *Béatitudes*, après s'être soigneusement enquis du jour qui pouvait convenir au ministre des beaux-arts et avoir invité par démarches personnelles les critiques des grands journaux, le directeur du Conservatoire et celui de l'Opéra.

Les *soli* étaient confiés à des élèves de chant du Conservatoire; quant aux chœurs, composés de vingt personnes environ, c'était les disciples particuliers du maître joints à ceux de sa classe d'orgue qui remplissaient les fonctions de choristes.

Franck, plein de joie de cette exécution au petit pied, devait accompagner lui-même au pi-

personally sought out and invited the critics on the leading papers, the Director of the Conservatoire and the Director of the Opéra.

The solo parts were confided to voice pupils from the Conservatoire; and the chorus, consisting of about twenty, was made up of Franck's private pupils together with some from his organ classes.

Franck was filled with delight at the prospect of this little performance, and intended to play the piano part himself; but two days before the appointed time he sprained his wrist while closing a carriage door, and it was to me that he entrusted the task of performing the piano reduction of the orchestral score to his selected guests, upon whose approval he was depending so absolutely.

All was in readiness, none of the participants was missing, and we only awaited the arrival of the guests, when a message was brought from the Minister, expressing much regret that he was unable to be present, etc. The Directors both of the Conservatoire and of the Opéra had already sent their excuses. As for the leading critics, they were kept away by a duty much more pressing than to give a hearing to an oratorio by a man of genius—they had to attend the opening performance of an operetta in a women's theatre! Some of them did indeed put in an appearance, only to leave almost immediately, and there were only two of the listeners who remained until the end: Edouard Lalo and Victorien Joncières did yield to Franck that mark of respect. But from this audition, which he had promised himself was to bring such good fortune, poor Franck turned away sad and somewhat disillusioned; not that he doubted the beauty of his score, but because every one, and even we his friends (who have said our *mea culpa*), made no effort to conceal our opinion that a performance of the complete work was impossible. He had, however, made up his mind, though with some bitterness, to divide the oratorio into sections; and it was thus that he offered it to the Société des Concerts du Conservatoire, which made him wait a long while before they admitted even one of the eight parts to its programmes.

ano, mais l'avant-veille du jour fixé, il se foula le poignet en fermant une portière de voiture et ce fut à moi qu'il confia le soin de présenter aux hôtes de choix sur l'appui desquels il comptait si absolument, la réduction d'orchestre de son œuvre qu'il me fallut apprendre en une journée.

Tout était prêt, aucun des exécutants ne manquait à l'appel, on n'attendait pour commencer que l'arrivée des invités lorsque survint un message du ministre exprimant "tous ses regrets de ne pouvoir se rendre à la soirée, etc., etc. . . ." Les directeurs de l'Opéra et du Conservatoire s'étaient excusés d'avance; quant aux grands critiques, ils étaient pris par un devoir autrement important que l'audition d'un oratorio de génie: on donnait, ce soir-là, dans un théâtre à femmes, la première représentation d'une opérette! . . . Quelques journalistes vinrent cependant se montrer pour se retirer presqu'aussitôt; il n'y eut que deux invités qui persistèrent à rester jusqu'à la fin; Edouard Lalo et Victorin de Joncières tinrent à donner à Franck cette marque de déférence. Mais, de cette audition dont il s'était promis tant de bonheur, le pauvre Franck sortit triste et un peu désillusionné, non point qu'il doutât de la beauté de son œuvre, mais parceque tous, et nous-mêmes, ses amis,—nous en faisons maintenant notre *mea culpa*—ne lui avions point caché qu'une exécution intégrale des *Béatitudes* au concert nous paraissait impossible; il avait donc pris, quoiqu'un peu amèrement, son parti de débiter la partition par *tranches;* c'est ainsi qu'il la présenta à la Société des Concerts du Conservatoire qui lui fit longuement attendre l'admission de l'une des huit parties à ses programmes.

Quatorze ans plus tard, Colonne, qui avait une revanche à prendre de l'étranglement de *Rédemption*, montait avec un grand soin et un réel souci du *rendu* artistique, l'oratorio des *Béatitudes* dans son entier. L'effet en fut foudroyant et le nom de Franck fut dès ce moment entouré d'une auréole de gloire qui ne fit que gagner en éclat, mais, depuis trois ans déjà, le maître était mort. . . .

A la suite de la malencontreuse audition pri-

Fourteen years later, Colonne, who wished to have his revenge for the strangling of *Le Rédemption*, performed with great care and a real desire for an artistic rendition the oratorio of *Les Béatitudes* in its entirety. The effect was overwhelming, and from that moment the name of Franck was surrounded by a halo of glory, growing ever more refulgent; but the great master had already been dead three years.

Following the unfortunate private hearing which has been mentioned above, the Minister of Fine Arts, who was perhaps a little remorseful, endeavored to have César Franck appointed one of the instructors in composition at the Conservatoire in the position left vacant by the death of Reber; but it was the composer of *Madame Turlupin*, Ernest Guiraud, who was preferred to the composer of *Les Béatitudes*.

On the other hand, and as a sort of compensation, the Government conferred a distinction upon the master; he was raised, together with bootmakers, tailors and every sort of purveyor to official needs, to the high honor of an Officier d'Académie!! Some years later, in 1886, Franck did indeed receive the ribbon of a Chevalier de la Légion d'honneur; but it would be a mistake to imagine that this distinction was conferred upon the composer whose many works have brought glory to French music—not at all; it was to the *official* who had completed more than ten years of routine service that the Cross was awarded, and the "Journal Officiel" merely makes the following statement: Franck (César Auguste), *professor of music*. The French Government was decidedly maladroit in its dealings with our composer!

The last four years of Franck's life witnessed the completion of four masterpieces which remain as beacon lights in the history of French composition: the Sonata for piano and violin, dedicated to Ysaye, the Symphony in D minor, the Quartet for strings, and the Suite of three chorales for organ, which was his last composition.

The symphony was performed by the Société des Concerts du Conservatoire in February,

vée dont il a été fait mention plus haut, le ministre des beaux-arts, poursuivi peut-être par un remords, tenta de faire attribuer à César Franck l'une des classes de composition du Conservatoire, devenue vacante par la mort de Reber, mais, à l'auteur des *Béatitudes*, ce fut l'auteur de *Madame Turlupin*, Ernest Guiraud, qui fut préféré.

Par contre, et en guise de compensation, une faveur fut accordée au maître par le gouvernement, on l'éleva, concurremment avec les bottiers, tailleurs et fournisseurs de tout ordre des gens officiels, à la haute dignité *d'officier d'académie!!* Quelques années plus tard, en 1886, Franck reçut enfin le ruban de Chevalier de la Légion d'honneur, mais on se tromperait en pensant que cette distinction fut déférée au musicien, auteur de tant d'œuvres qui honorent l'art français, point du tout! c'est au *fonctionnaire ayant plus de dix ans de service* que la croix fut attribuée et le Journal officiel porte seulement la mention: Franck (César Auguste) *professeur de musique.* — Le gouvernement français avait décidément avec lui la main malheureuse!

Les quatre dernières années de la vie du maître virent l'éclosion de quatre chefs d'œuvre qui resteront comme des points lumineux dans l'histoire de notre art, ce sont: la Sonate pour piano et violon dédiée aux Ysaye, la Symphonie en *ré*, le Quatuor à cordes et la suite de trois Chorals pour orgue qui fut son dernier chant.

La Symphonie fut exécutée par la Société des concerts du Conservatoire en février 1889, contre le gré de la plupart des membres du célèbre orchestre et grâce seulement à l'amicale opiniâtreté de son chef, Jules Garcin. Les abonnés n'y comprirent quoique ce soit, les musiciens officiels pas davantage. L'un d'eux, professeur au Conservatoire et membre influent du Comité des Concerts, auquel j'exprimais mon admiration pour l'œuvre et pour l'exécution, me répondit dédaigneusement: "Ça, une symphonie? . . . Mais, cher Monsieur, on n'écrit pas de cor anglais dans une symphonie! en trouvez-vous seulement dans les symphonies d'Haydn? Non, n'est-ce pas? Vous voyez donc bien que cette musique de votre Franck, ce n'est *pas même une*

1889, contrary to the wish of most of the players in that celebrated orchestra, and chiefly thanks to the amiable pertinacity of their conductor, Jules Garcin. The subscribers had no idea what it was all about, and professional musicians had but little more. One of them, a professor at the Conservatoire and an influential member of the Comité des Concerts, to whom I expressed my admiration for the work and for its performance, answered me scornfully, "That a symphony? But, my dear sir, one does n't write for English horn in a symphony. Do you find it, for instance, in the symphonies of Haydn? No, of course not. So you see that this music of your friend Franck is not even a symphony!" At another door of the concert hall the composer of *Faust* and *Mireille*, surrounded by a bevy of admirers, especially of the gentler sex, declared pontifically that the symphony was "the assertion of incapacity carried almost to the point of dogma." Gounod should expiate these words in some musical purgatory; for, coming from a composer of his quality, they could not have been sincere.

Played triumphantly all over the world by Eugène Ysaye, the violin sonata was to Franck a source of unalloyed joy; but he was greatly astonished by the success, then without precedent, of his string quartet at one of the concerts of the Société Nationale de Musique, although he was one of the founders of that society, and had been elected its president several years previously.

At the first performance of the quartet, the members of the Société Nationale, whose education toward works in the new manner was already in progress, were seized with an enthusiasm as sincere as it was contagious. In the Salle Pleyel, ringing with applause, all those present remained on their feet, shouting and calling for the composer who, not being able to imagine such a success for a string quartet, insisted upon believing that this demonstration was intended for the players. However, when he appeared, shy, smiling, amazed, upon the platform (in those days a composer was very rarely called out), he could not doubt for a moment that the delirium

symphonie !" — A une autre issue de la salle des concerts, l'auteur de *Faust* et de *Mireille*, entouré d'un cortège d'adulateurs et surtout d'adulatrices, déclarait pontificalement que cette symphonie était *"l'affirmation de l'impuissance poussée jusqu'au dogme."* . . . Gounod doit expier, dans quelque purgatoire musical, cette parole qui, de la part d'un musicien comme lui, ne *pouvait* pas être sincère.

La Sonate qu'Eugène Ysaye promena triomphalement à travers le monde, fut pour Franck la source de pures joies, mais le plus grand de ses étonnements fut causé par le succès, alors sans précédent, de son Quatuor à cordes à l'un des concerts de la *Société nationale de musique* qu'il avait contribué à fonder et dont il avait été nommé président depuis quelques années.

Lors de la première audition de ce quatuor, les membres de la Société nationale, dont l'éducation vers les œuvres de forme nouvelle commençait à se faire, furent saisis d'un enthousiasme aussi sincère que communicatif; dans la salle Pleyel, vibrante d'applaudissements, tous les assistants étaient debout, acclamant, appelant le maître qui, ne pouvant imaginer un tel succès pour un quatuor, s'obstinait à croire que ces manifestations s'addressaient aux interprètes. Cependant, lorsque timide, souriant, étonné, il reparut sur l'estrade (à cette époque, il était bien rare qu'on rappelât des auteurs), il ne put douter un seul instant que ce délire causé par son œuvre fut bien à son adresse, et, le lendemain, tout fier de ce premier succès (à 68 ans!), il nous disait naïvement: "Allons, voilà le public qui commence à me comprendre. . . ."

Mais cette douce impression fut de courte durée, car, en l'été de 1890, dans une de ses courses pédestres et hâtives à travers Paris, distrait peut-être par la recherche de quelque idée musicale, il ne sut pas se garer à temps du choc d'un omnibus dont le timon le frappa au côté. Insoucieux de la douleur physique, le maître continua de mener sa vie ordinaire de labeurs et de fatigues, mais bientôt, une grave pleurésie s'étant déclarée, il fut forcé de s'aliter et succomba le 8 novembre 1890.

caused by his quartet was intended for himself; and the following day, proud of his first success (at the age of sixty-eight!), he said to us naïvely, "Well, you see the public begins to understand me."

These agreeable impressions were to be his but a short time to enjoy, for during the summer of 1890, while taking one of his early walks about Paris and perhaps preoccupied with some musical idea, he failed to avoid collision with an omnibus and the pole struck him in the side. Disregarding his physical pain, he continued to lead his ordinary life of fatiguing work; but soon a serious pleurisy developed; he had to take to his bed and finally succumbed to the disease November 8, 1890.

Only a short time before his death he wished to drag himself again to his organ at Sainte Clotilde in order to indicate the registration of his three organ chorales which, like Bach one hundred and thirty years before, he left as a splendid legacy to the world of music.

His funeral ceremony was simple, as his life had been. By special authorization the services took place not in his own parish of Saint Jacques but in the basilica of Sainte Clotilde, where for thirty years he had chanted almost daily the glory of God. Canon Gardey, rector of Sainte Clotilde, who had administered the last rites of the church to Franck on his deathbed, delivered from the pulpit an eloquent oration; then, without pomp or ceremony, the cortège proceeded to the cemetery of Montrouge, where the remains were interred in a remote corner.[1]

There was no official delegation either from the Minister of Fine Arts or from its personnel to accompany Franck's body to its last resting-place. Even the Conservatoire de Musique, in whose corps of instructors he was included; the Conservatoire, whose directors ordinarily let slip no opportunity to present themselves at the customary public ceremonies around the tomb of some empirical singing-teacher or some ob-

Bien peu de temps avant sa mort, il avait voulu se traîner encore à son orgue de Sainte Clotilde afin de combiner et d'écrire la régistration des trois Chorals pour orgue, que, tel Sébastien Bach cent trente ans auparavant, il laissa comme un sublime testament musical.

Simples comme sa vie furent ses obsèques; le service eut lieu, par autorisation spéciale, non à Saint Jacques, sa paroisse, mais en cette basilique de Sainte Clotilde où il chantait, presque journellement depuis trente ans, les gloires du Seigneur.

M. le chanoine Gardey, curé titulaire de la basilique, qui lui avait, à ses derniers moments, apporté les secours spirituels de la religion, prononça, en chaire, un émouvant éloge funèbre, puis, sans faste ni apparat, le cortège se dirigea vers le cimetière de Montrouge où la dépouille du maître fut inhumée en un coin très reculé.[1]

Aucune délégation officielle du ministère ni de l'administration des beaux-arts ne l'accompagna à sa demeure dernière; le Conservatoire de musique lui-même, qui le comptait cependant au nombre des membres de son corps enseignant, le Conservatoire, dont les directeurs s'empressent d'ordinaire de venir débiter de traditionnels lieux communs sur la tombe d'empiriques professeurs de chant ou d'obscurs moniteurs de solfège, le Conservatoire négligea de se faire représenter à la cérémonie funèbre de son unique professeur d'orgue dont les hautes théories d'art avaient toujours semblé un danger pour la quiétude de l'établissement officiel.

Seuls, les nombreux élèves du maître, ses amis, les musiciens que son affabilité sans bornes avait su attirer à lui, formèrent une couronne de respectueuse admiration autour du cercueil.

César Franck, en mourant, avait légué à son pays d'adoption une école symphonique pleine de vie et de sève créatrice, telle que jamais jusqu'alors la France n'en avait produit.

Et c'est avec une grande justesse de prévisions qu'Emmanuel Chabrier (qui devait si peu

_____

[1] _They were disinterred some years later, and moved to the Cimetière Montparnasse, where a monument adorned with a medallion by Auguste Rodin was erected through the efforts of the composer's friends and pupils._

[1] _Elle fut exhumée quelques années plus tard et transférée au cimetière Montparnasse, où un monument funéraire orné d'un médaillon d'Auguste Rodin fut érigé par les soins des élèves et des amis au maître._

scure professor of solfeggio;—even the Conservatoire neglected to send any representative to the obsequies of its truly great organ teacher, whose noble ideals of his art had always seemed dangerous to the academic quiet of that institution.

The many pupils of the master, his friends, those musicians who had become attached to him through his unlimited geniality—these alone formed a crown of love and admiration about his grave.

César Franck in dying had bequeathed to the country of his adoption a symphonic school full of life and creative vigor, such as France up to that time had never produced.

And it was with most accurate prevision that Emmanuel Chabrier (who survived him so brief a time) concluded in the following words the very affecting eulogy which he delivered at the tomb on behalf of the Société Nationale de Musique: "Farewell, O Master, and thanks—your task was well done. It is one of the greatest geniuses of the century whom we salute in you: it is also the incomparable teacher whose marvellous precepts have produced an entire generation of sturdy musicians, thoughtful and consecrated, armed at all points for the righteous battle, however long it may be waged. And to the honorable and upright man, so kindly and unselfish, who never spoke aught but good, and who always gave wise counsel—to him also, Farewell."

Fourteen years after this intimate and affectionate funeral ceremony, the same pupils, the same friends, the same musicians — somewhat decimated, alas! by death—came together again in the square which faces the basilica of Sainte Clotilde, to dedicate the monument erected by subscription to the memory of the beloved composer; but this time an enthusiastic crowd surrounded them, this time official dignitaries occupied prominent places, and both the Minister of Fine Arts and the Director of the Conservatoire delivered eloquent orations. What had happened during these fourteen years? Very quietly and almost unheeded the name of César Franck, but

lui survivre) termina en ces termes l'allocution très émue qu'il prononça sur la tombe au nom de la Société nationale de musique:

"Adieu, maître, et merci, car vous avez bien fait. C'est un des plus grands artistes de ce siècle que nous saluons en vous; c'est aussi le professeur incomparable dont le merveilleux enseignement a fait éclore toute une génération de musiciens robustes, croyants et réfléchis, armés de toutes pièces pour les combats sévères souvent longuement disputés. C'est aussi l'homme juste et droit, si humain et si désintéressé qui ne donna jamais que le sûr conseil et la bonne parole.—Adieu!"

.   .   .   .

Quatorze ans après ces intimes et affectueuses funérailles, les mêmes disciples, les mêmes amis, les mêmes musiciens, un peu décimés, hélas! par la mort, se retrouvaient réunis dans le square qui fait face à la basilique de Sainte Clotilde, dans le but d'inaugurer un monument élevé par souscription à la mémoire du maître aimé; mais cette fois, une foule enthousiaste s'était jointe à eux, cette fois, les gens officiels avaient tenu à figurer aux places d'honneur et le directeur des beaux-arts, ainsi que celui du Conservatoire lui-même, y firent des discours très remarqués. . . . Que s'était-il donc passé de nouveau dans ces quatorze années? Tout doucement et sans qu'on y ait pris garde, le nom de César Franck, naguère vénéré par de rares croyants, était devenu célèbre. Alors, cette administration, ce Conservatoire, qui, de son vivant, avaient méconnu le modeste professeur d'orgue, s'empressèrent de le réclamer comme leur. . . .

Alors, nombre ne jeunes compositeurs qui auraient craint de se compromettre en allant lui demander des conseils, se trouvèrent, comme par enchantement, avoir été ses élèves. . . .

L'Institut de France ne put toutefois se faire représenter à l'inauguration de ce monument, car, tandis qu'il accueillait dans son sein de flagrantes non-valeurs, comme l'auteur des *Noces de Jeannette* ou celui du *Voyage en Chine*, pour ne citer que des morts, il ne sut point ouvrir ses portes à l'un des plus grands musiciens qui aient honoré notre pays de France.

lately revered by a few disciples, had become renowned. Therefore the Fine Arts and the Conservatoire, which during his lifetime had ig-
nored the modest organ professor, hastened to
claim him as their own.

And several young composers who had feared
lest they might jeopardize themselves by going
to him for instruction discovered as by enchant-
ment that they had been numbered among his
pupils.

The Institut de France could not, however,
be represented at the dedication of this monument; for whereas it had welcomed to its bosom
such conspicuous mediocrities as the composer
of *Les Noces de Jeannette* or the writer of *Le
Voyage en Chine,* to mention only those who are
no longer living, it had never opened its doors
to one of the greatest musicians who had ever
brought honor to our France.

And this just reversal of public opinion is the
more securely established as it is not founded
upon sterile intrigue or the effort to reach an
ephemeral success, but rests solely on the sincerity and the immortal beauty of works that remain
as an example to all who would make themselves
worthy to bear the noble name of composer.

Et ce juste retour de l'opinion est d'autant
plus solidement établi qu'il n'a point pour base
l'intrigue inféconde ou l'éphémère appel au succès, mais seulement la sincérité et l'immortelle
beauté d'un œuvre laissé en exemple à tous ceux
qui veulent se rendre digne du noble nom d'artiste créateur.

II

In physical appearance Franck was short of
stature; he had a high forehead, an animated and
open expression, though his eyes were almost
buried under the sheltering brows; the nose was
rather large, and the chin retreated under a wide
and extraordinarily expressive mouth. His face
was round, and this was accentuated by luxuri-
ant whiskers, which were turning gray.

Such was the figure which we loved and hon-
ored for twenty years, and which, except for the
whitening of the hair, changed scarcely at all till
his death.

Certainly there was nothing in his appearance
which seemed to indicate the artist, or which con-
formed to the type created by romantic legends
coupled with the traditions of Montmartre. Who,
indeed, encountering in the street that individ-

Au physique, Franck était de petite taille; il
avait le front haut, le regard vif et loyal, bien que
ses yeux fussent comme enfouis sous l'arcade
sourcilière; le nez un peu fort, le menton fuyant
sous une large bouche extraordinairement expressive, le visage de forme ronde, encore élargi par
des favoris grisonnants et très fournis.

Telle est la figure que nous avons honorée
et aimée pendant vingt ans et qui, sauf le blan-
chissement de la chevelure, ne changea point
jusqu'à sa mort.

Au total, rien dans cet aspect qui paraisse ré-
véler *l'artiste* conforme au type que les légendes
romantiques aussi bien que les légendes montmar-
troises se complurent à créer; aussi, quiconque
coudoyait dans la rue cet être toujours pressé
trottant plutôt que marchant, la physionomie

ual always in haste, trotting rather than walk-
ing, with a preoccupied expression and frequent
grimaces, clothed in a coat too large and in
trousers too short, could have imagined the transformation which took place when, at the piano,
he explained or commented upon some piece of
beautiful music; or still more when, with one
hand to his forehead and the other arrested
in the direction of the stops, he sat at the organ
making ready for one of his charming improvisations? Then did music seem to envelop him
entirely as with an aureole; then only was one
struck by the purposeful firmness of the mouth
and chin, by the almost superhuman keenness
of the eyes in whose light gleamed inspiration;
then only one noticed the almost perfect resemblance of his fine and broad brow to that of the
composer of the Ninth Symphony; and one
could scarcely avoid feeling a sort of supersti-
tious awe in the presence of the genius which
illumined the countenance, so surpassingly fine
and noble, of the greatest musician produced by
France during the nineteenth century.

The quality which predominated above all
others in Franck's nature was his capacity for
work. Winter and summer he arose at about
half-past five every morning. He generally devoted the first two hours of the day to composition, which he called working for himself. At
about half-past seven, after a frugal breakfast,
he started out to give lessons in every corner of
the capital; for, almost up to the end of his life,
this great man had to spend the greater part of
his time in giving piano lessons to amateurs in
the music departments of colleges and boarding-
schools. Thus all day long he travelled about,
on foot or by omnibus, from Auteuil to the Isle
Saint Louis, from Vaugiraud to the Faubourg
Poissonière; and he did not usually return to
his quiet apartment in the Boulevard Saint Michel until it was time for the evening meal. Although fatigued by his day of toil, he still could
find a few moments for copying or orchestrating
his scores, when he did not devote the evening
to receiving his pupils in organ or composition
and lavishing upon them valuable and disinter-

distraite et perpétuellement grimaçante, et vêtu
de redingotes trop larges et de pantalons trop
courts, ne pouvait soupçonner la transfiguration
qui s'opérait en lui lorsqu'il expliquait ou com-
mentait au piano une belle œuvre d'art, ou bien
encore lorsque, une main à son front et l'autre
comme en arrêt vers la combinaison des régis-
tres, il préparait à l'orgue l'une de ses géniales
improvisations. Alors, la musique l'enveloppait
tout entier comme une auréole, alors seulement,
on était frappé par la volonté consciente de la
bouche et du menton, par l'acuité presque sur-
humaine des yeux au travers desquels transparais-
sait l'inspiration, alors seulement on remarquait
l'identité presque complète du pur et large front
avec celui du créateur de la *IXe Symphonie* et l'on ne
pouvait se défendre d'une sorte d'effroi presque
superstitieux au contact du génie rayonnant autour de la plus haute et de la plus noble figure de
musicien qu'ait produit notre XIXe siècle français.

Au moral, ce qui frappait tout d'abord chez
Franck, c'était la puissance de travail. Hiver
comme été, on le trouvait debout dès cinq heures
et demi du matin; il consacrait généralement les
deux premières heures de la matinée à la composition, c'est ce qu'il appelait: travailler *pour lui;*
vers sept heures et demi, après un frugal déjeu-
ner, il partait pour aller donner des leçons dans
tous les coins de la capitale, car, jusqu'à la fin
de sa vie, ce grand homme dut consacrer la plus
grande partie de son temps à l'éducation pianis-
tique de quelques amateurs, voire à des cours de
musique dans des collèges ou des pensionnats.

C'est ainsi que, toute la journée, il se trans-
porte à pied ou en omnibus, d'Auteuil à l'Ile
Saint-Louis, de Vaugirard au faubourg Poisson-
nière; il ne regagne d'ordinaire son calme logis
du boulevard Saint Michel que pour le repas du
soir, et, bien que fatigué de sa journée de labeur,
il trouve encore quelques instants pour copier ou
orchestrer ses partitions, quand il ne consacre pas
sa soirée à recevoir ses élèves d'orgue ou de composition et à leur prodiguer des conseils précieux
et désintéressés. C'est donc pendant ses deux
heures de travail matinal jointes aux quelques
semaines de vacances que lui laissait sa situation

ested counsel. But it was during his two hours of work in the early morning, coupled with the few weeks of vacation which his position at the Conservatoire allowed him, that his greatest and most beautiful compositions were created, planned and written.

If Franck was a stubborn worker, it was not that, as a result of his labors, he sought in any way for glory, profit or an immediate success. On the contrary, his only desire was to express his thoughts and emotions as ably as he might, and to give his best to the art that he loved; for he was above everything else modest.

Never had he known that feverish desire which gnaws at the very existence of so many artists; I mean the lust for honors and advancement. It never occurred to him, for example, to aspire to the chair of a Member of the Institut; not at all because, like Degas and Puvis de Chavannes, he disdained the title, but because he innocently thought he had not accomplished enough to deserve it!

This modesty did not, however, exclude that quality of self-confidence which is so important to the creative artist when it rests upon sober judgment and is free of vanity. When, at the opening of the autumn session, the master, with his face illumined by his generous smile, would say to us confidentially, "I have done *good* work during my vacation, I believe you will be pleased," we were sure that presently some masterpiece would be disclosed.

His joy was to find in his full life some hours of an evening when he might assemble his favorite pupils and play for them at the piano some newly completed composition, aiding himself in the vocal portions by a voice as grotesque and uneven as it was expressive and warm. He never hesitated to ask his pupils' opinion of his work and even to adopt the suggestions they ventured to make, if they seemed to him well founded.

Unfailing industry, modesty and high artistic ideals — these were the salient points in Franck's character; but there was another quality which is rare enough, and perhaps rarest among artists, which he possessed in a supreme degree — the

au Conservatoire, que furent pensées, disposées et écrites ses plus belles œuvres.

Mais si Franck fut un travailleur opiniâtre, ce n'est point qu'il cherchait dans le résultat de son travail gloire, profit ou succès immédiat, bien loin de là, il ne prétendit jamais à autrechose qu'à exprimer de son mieux ses pensées et ses sentiments à l'aide de son art, car c'était avant tout un modeste.

Jamais il ne connut cet état de fièvre qui ronge l'existence de tant d'artistes, je veux parler de la course aux honneurs et aux distinctions; jamais il ne lui vint, par exemple, l'idée de briguer le fauteuil de Membre de l'Institut, non point que, comme un Degas ou un Puvis de Chavannes, il dédaignat ce titre, mais parce qu'il pensait naïvement n'avoir point assez fait pour le mériter!

Cette modestie n'excluait pourtant pas chez lui la *confiance en soi*, si importante pour l'artiste créateur lorsqu'elle est appuyée sur un jugement sain et exempt de vanité. Lorsqu'à l'automne, à l'ouverture des cours, le maître, le visage illuminé par son large sourire, nous disait comme confidentiellement: " J'ai *bien* travaillé, ces vacances, je crois que vous serez contents!", nous étions certains de la prochaine éclosion de quelque chef-d'œuvre.

Alors, sa joie était de trouver dans son existence si occupée, quelques heures de soirée pour rassembler ses élèves de prédilection et leur jouer au piano l'œuvre nouvellement terminée, en s'aidant, pour les parties vocales, d'un organe aussi grotesque et inégal qu'il était expressif et chaleureux. Il ne dédaignait même point de demander à ses élèves leur avis sur l'œuvre et, bien mieux encore, de s'y conformer si les observations qu'osaient faire ceux-ci lui paraissaient bien fondées.

Assiduité constante dans le travail, modestie et conscience artistique, tels étaient les points saillants du caractère de Franck; mais il est encore une qualité, bien rare, celle-là, peut-être surtout chez les artistes, qu'il posséda au suprême degré, ce fut la bonté, l'indulgente et sereine bonté.

Il ne faudrait pas cependant inférer de là que le maître fut d'un tempérament froid et placide,

quality of goodness, forgiving and indulgent goodness.

It must not be inferred that the master was of a cool and placid temperament; on the contrary, his was a passionate nature, and all his works give evidence of this. Who among us does not remember his holy wrath against vulgar music, his impatient start when the bell at the altar forced him to end too abruptly an interestingly developed *offertoire*, his torrential invectives when at the organ our awkward fingers strayed toward faulty combinations? But these passionate outbursts of the *méridional du nord* generally had for their object some artistic principle, they were very seldom directed toward any person; and during the long years which I spent at his side I have never heard it said that he had in any way consciously given pain to any one. How could he ever have done so, since his soul was incapable of conceiving anything evil? Never would he believe in the base jealousies which his genius provoked among his *confrères* (and not among those of least reputation); for he passed through life with his eyes lifted to a high ideal, and was always unwilling to give credence to the inherent failings of human nature, to which, unfortunately, those of artistic aptitudes are far from being immune.

Franck drew his strength and goodness from his religion, for he was very devout; with him, as with all who are truly great, belief in his art was associated with faith in God, the source of all beauty. Some ill-informed critics endeavored to compare the Jesus, so divinely loving and compassionate, of *Les Béatitudes* to the sorrowful weakling depicted under that name by Ernest Renan — certainly these gentlemen have never understood the music of Franck, and most completely would they have been undeceived if, like some of us who were admitted to the gallery of Sainte Clotilde, they had been permitted to join in the act of devotion so simply performed by the master each Sunday when, at the Consecration, he interrupted his improvisation and, leaving the organ-bench, went to the corner of the gallery to kneel in fervent adoration before God present on the altar.

Franck was religious, as were Palestrina, Bach

tant s'en faut, c'était un passionné et, certes, toutes ses œuvres en font foi. Qui de nous ne se souvient de ses saintes colères contre la mauvaise musique, de ses soubresauts d'impatience lorsque la sonnette de l'autel le forçait de terminer trop brusquement un *offertoire* bien exposé, de ses tonitruantes apostrophes quand nos doigts malhabiles s'égaraient, à l'orgue, en de fautives combinaisons? Mais ces emportements de *méridional du nord* avaient généralement pour objet des *principes* d'art, ils s'adressaient bien rarement à des personnes et, pendant les longues années vécues à ses côtés, je n'ai point entendu dire qu'il ait, en quoi que ce soit, fait sciemment de la peine à quelqu'un. Comment cela aurait-il pu être, puisque son âme était inapte à concevoir le mal? Jamais il ne voulut croire aux basses jalousies que son talent suscitait parmi ses collègues (et non les moins réputés); il passa dans la vie les yeux levés vers un très haut idéal, sans vouloir soupçonner les vilenies inhérentes à la nature humaine dont la gent artiste est malheureusement bien loin d'être exempte.

Cette force et cette bonté, c'était dans sa *foi* que Franck les puisait, car il était profondément croyant; chez lui, comme chez tous les *très grands*, la foi en son art se confondait avec la foi en Dieu, source de tout art. Quelques critiques bien mal informés ont voulu comparer le Jésus si divinement aimant et miséricordieux des *Béatitudes* au triste bellâtre présenté sous ce nom par Ernest Renan; ces gens n'ont certainement jamais rien compris à l'œuvre de Franck et, à coup sûr, ils eussent été détrompés, si, comme ceux d'entre nous qui étaient admis à la tribune de Sainte Clotilde, ils avaient pu assister à l'acte de foi très simplement accompli chaque dimanche par le maître, alors qu'au moment de la Consécration, il interrompait l'improvisation commencée et que, descendant les degrés de l'orgue, il allait au coin de la tribune s'incliner en une fervente adoration devant le Dieu de l'autel.

Croyant, Franck le fut, comme un Palestrina, un Bach, un Beethoven; confiant en l'autre vie, il ne rabaissa point son art dans le but d'obtenir en celle-ci une vaine gloire, il eut la sincérité naïve

and Beethoven—having faith in a future life, he never debased his gift to seek therefrom a vain renown, he possessed the simple honesty of true genius. And while the ephemeral vogue of many composers who labored merely to acquire fame or to win fortune has commenced surely to retreat into a shadow whence it will never return, the seraphic figure of him who wrote *Les Béatitudes*, and who composed purely for music's sake, ascends ever higher in the light toward which, without compromise or cessation, he directed his entire life.

du génie. Aussi, tandis que l'éphémère renommée de bien des compositeurs qui ne travaillèrent que pour acquérir la fortune ou obtenir le succès, commence actuellement à entrer dans l'ombre pour n'en plus sortir jamais, la figure séraphique de l'auteur des *Béatitudes*, qui travailla pour l'Art uniquement, plane de plus en plus haut dans la lumière vers laquelle, sans compromissions ni défaillances, il s'est dirigé toute sa vie.

III

THIS is not the place to study the work of Franck in its entirety; but I wish, nevertheless, to mention his most important productions and to show the marked influence which he exerted upon the development of French composition at the close of the nineteenth century. Like that of all great composers whose history is pretty well known, the compositions of César Franck may be assigned to three very definite periods, differing widely in style.

The first occupied the years from 1841 to 1855, and it includes the four trios, all the early piano pieces, several songs, and culminates notably with his first oratorio, *Ruth*.

The second period lasted from 1858 to 1872; it may be termed the epoch of religious composition, properly so called, including masses, motets and organ pieces, and concludes with the second oratorio, *Le Rédemption*.

The third period witnessed the production of all the orchestra music, beginning with 1875: *Les Eolides* (1876), *Le Chasseur maudit* (1883), *Les Djinns* (1884), the *Variations symphoniques* (1885), *Psyché* (1888), and the Symphony in D minor (1889). Also the following chamber music: the Quintet in F minor (1880), the Sonata for violin (1886), and the Quartet for strings (1889). Included further are the two operas, *Hulda* (1879–82) and *Ghisèle* (1888–90), performed at Monte Carlo in 1894 and 1896 respectively; the three organ Chorales (1890); and finally the superb choral epic, *Les Béatitudes* (1869–80).

CE n'est pas ici le lieu d'étudier l'œuvre de Franck dans son ensemble, je veux néanmoins, avant de parler de son œuvre de piano, énumérer au moins ses principales productions et montrer la décisive influence qu'il exerça sur l'orientation de la musique française à la fin du XIXe siècle. Comme celle de tous les grands artistes dont la vie fut quelque peu étendue, la carrière de César Franck peut se diviser en trois époques très tranchées et très différentes dans leurs résultats.

La première s'étend de 1841 vers 1855 et comprend les quatre trios, toutes les premières pièces pour piano, un certain nombre de mélodies, et aboutit comme point saillant à son premier oratorio: *Ruth*.

La seconde période va de 1858 à 1872; c'est l'époque de la production religieuse proprement dite: Messes, motets, pièces d'orgue; elle se termine au second oratorio: *Rédemption*.

La dernière manière comprend toute la musique d'orchestre à partir de 1875: Les *Eolides* (1876), le *Chasseur maudit* (1883), les *Djinns* (1884), les *Variations symphoniques* (1885), *Psyché* (1888), la *Symphonie en ré* (1889); la musique de chambre: *Quintette en fa mineur* (1880), *Sonate pour violon* (1886), *Quatuor à cordes* (1889); les deux opéras: *Hulda* (1879–1882) et *Ghisèle* (1888–1890), représentés au théâtre de Monte-Carlo en 1894 et 1896, les trois chorals d'orgue (1890); et enfin l'admirable épopée des *Béatitudes* (1869–1880).

Chez tous les grands hommes, que ce soit

With all great men, such as Gluck, Rembrandt, Beethoven, Puvis, Goethe and Wagner, the last manner is always the one which gives birth to the finest works, to masterpieces which remain permanent contributions to the history of art. It was not otherwise with Franck; and fortunately that period coincided with the moment when, by virtue of his official position and his artistic reputation already established, he was able to impart to a host of youthful spirits the lofty canons of an art which at that time was not to be found in France. If one studies with the kindest intentions the productions of French composers prior to 1870 in the domain of the symphony, or more especially in the realm of chamber music, what does one find after industrious search? The works of Onslow, an insipid collection of quartets that aged in their own day, and of quintets adaptable to any instruments; a few pieces by Félicien David and by Ambroise Thomas, and even some poor quartets by Gounod—composers who were all too engrossed in the opera house to write absolute music with the conviction necessary to produce a beautiful work.

In 1871 a group of composers, young for the most part, in the forefront of whom we find Saint-Saëns, Fauré, Duparc and Castillon, founded the Société Nationale de Musique with the object of fostering French composition in all fields. After some years Franck was elected president of the society, and immediately began to gather about him all the musicians of our country who viewed their art as something other than an accessory of the theatre.

If the master exercised upon his contemporaries an undeniable influence, it is because he revealed himself to all musicians who had the privilege of approaching him, not only as a safe and certain guide, a teacher of the first rank, but as a *father*; and I do not hesitate to use that word to characterize him who brought the day of the French symphonic school. All of us, his pupils, with instinctive and unanimous, though unpremeditated, accord never called him by any other name than "le père Franck."

And so, while other professors of composition

Gluck, Rembrandt, Beethoven, Puvis, Goethe ou Wagner, la dernière manière est toujours celle qui donne naissance aux plus grandes œuvres, aux chefs-d'œuvres qui restent définitivement dans l'histoire de l'art. Il n'en fut pas autrement chez Franck et, par bonheur, cette période coïncida avec le moment où, par sa position officielle et sa réputation artistique déjà établie, il fut à même de répandre sur une multitude de jeunes esprits le haut enseignement d'art qu'il était alors impossible de rencontrer en France. Que l'on veuille bien examiner de bonne foi les essais des compositeurs français antérieurs à 1870 dans le genre symphonique et spécialement dans celui de la musique de chambre; que trouve-t-on, en cherchant bien? L'œuvre d'Onslow, insipide ramassis de quatuors vieillis avant l'âge et de quintettes *à tout faire* adaptables à tous les instruments, quelques rares pièces de Félicien David, d'Ambroise Thomas et même de très pauvres quatuors de Gounod, tous ces musiciens étaient bien trop inféodés au théâtre pour écrire de la musique pure avec la réelle conviction de tenter une belle œuvre.

En 1871, un groupe de compositeurs, jeunes pour la plupart, à la tête desquels on trouve Saint-Saens, Fauré, Duparc et Castillon, fondent la *Société nationale de musique* destinée à encourager la production française dans tous les genres. Au bout de peu d'années Franck est appelé à la présidence de cette Société et aussitôt viennent se serrer autour de lui tous les musiciens de notre pays qui envisagent leur art autrement que comme un prétexte à spectacle.

Si le maître exerça sur ses contemporains une indéniable influence, c'est qu'il se montra pour tous les artistes qui eurent le bonheur de l'approcher, non pas seulement un guide sûr et ferme, un éducateur de premier ordre, mais un *père*, et je ne crains pas de me servir de ce vocable pour caractériser celui qui donna le jour à l'école française de symphonie, car, nous, ses élèves, d'un accord instinctif et unanime, bien que non concerté, nous ne l'avons jamais nommé autrement que le *père Franck*.

of that day did no more than to correct the exercises brought to them, "le père Franck" alone knew how to hold his pupils by a genuine affection; he supported them morally in their difficult hours, he was indulgent toward their faults and he gave encouragement to their efforts. Moreover, it is a curious fact that this man, who had certainly nothing of the philosopher in him, was able to influence his young pupils in the way of practical psychology; for his simple goodness was a much better guide to him in such matters than any logic, and dictated the precise words which were of most value to his young friends in the very moment of their need, and this paternal psychology was of more benefit to his youthful disciples than any number of lessons in counterpoint or fugue.

However it happened, all, whether they wished it or no, felt the influence unconsciously exerted by that genial organist who loved music better than himself — first his associates in the Société Nationale, Lalo, Guilmant, Chabrier, Fauré, Castillon (who forsook his studies with Victor Massé to seek final instruction from the composer of *Le Rédemption*); then the students at the Conservatoire who were at some time in his organ classes, Samuel Rousseau, G. Pierné, A. Chapuis, G. Marty, Paul Vidal, Paul Dukas; and finally his private pupils in composition, A. Coquard, Henri Duparc, Pierre de Bréville, Ernest Chausson, Guy Ropartz, Louis de Serres, Augusta Holmès, Charles Bordes, Guillaume Lekeu, and the author of these lines. All preserved the indelible mark of their contact with the master; but far from seeking to form his pupils to his own image, like the professors at the Conservatoire, good Father Franck knew how to respect the individuality of those who studied under his guidance, and contented himself with the bestowal of instruction which was solidly based upon well-established laws.

Nevertheless, in spite of their actual dissimilarity and of qualities often the very opposite of each other, there is found in the compositions of all Franck's pupils a certain family resemblance, which is like the *cachet* of a sound education, and to which no discerning critic can be blind.

En effet, alors que tous les professeurs de composition de cette époque étaient de simples correcteurs de devoirs sans plus, le père Franck seul savait accueillir ses élèves avec une réelle affection, il les soutenait moralement dans les moments difficiles, indulgent aux faiblesses, encourageant aux efforts; et, chose curieuse, cet homme qui n'avait, certes, rien d'un philosophe, eut pu en remontrer à bien des théoriciens au point de vue de la psychologie pratique, car sa simple bonté, qui le guidait en cela bien mieux que tous les raisonnements, lui dictait les paroles précises à dire à un élève au moment précis où celui-ci en avait besoin, et cette paternelle psychologie fut plus efficace pour les jeunes vocations que de nombreuses leçons de fugue ou de contrepoint.

Quoiqu'il en soit, tous, qu'ils le veuillent ou non, subissent l'inconsciente influence de cet honnête organiste qui aime la musique plus que lui-même, ce sont d'abord ses collègues de la *Société nationale*, Lalo, Guilmant, Chabrier, Fauré, Castillon (qui répudia la direction de Victor Massé pour aller demander de définitifs conseils à l'auteur de *Rédemption*); puis les élèves du Conservatoire qui passèrent quelques temps dans sa classe d'orgue, Samuel Rousseau, G. Pierné, A. Chapuis, G. Marty, Paul Vidal, Paul Dukas; enfin ses véritables élèves de composition, A. Coquard, Henri Duparc, Pierre de Bréville, Ernest Chausson, Guy Ropartz, Louis de Serres, Augusta Holmès, Charles Bordes, Guillaume Lekeu et celui qui écrit ces lignes; tous gardent la trace indélébile de leur contact avec le maître; mais, bien loin de chercher, comme les professeurs du Conservatoire, à façonner ses élèves à sa propre image, le bon père Franck sait respecter la personnalité de ceux qui travaillent sous sa direction, se contentant de les doter d'une instruction solidement établie sur les principes traditionnels.

Et pourtant, malgré les divergences très réelles et les qualités souvent opposées de chacun, il reste dans toutes les productions des élèves de Franck un air de famille, comme un cachet de *bonne éducation* auquel nul critique clairvoyant ne peut se méprendre.

IV

WE come now to consideration of the piano compositions of César Franck.

It is a curious thing, and as far as I know not true of any other composer except the one we are discussing, that his compositions in this genre are found to be confined to the two extremes of his career. All the works of the first five years, from 1842 to 1846, except the four trios, consist of scarcely anything but piano pieces. Then Franck suddenly stopped completely for a period of fourteen years to write for the instrument beloved of Liszt and Chopin; and it is not till the closing five years of his life, from 1885 till his death, that he is haunted by the desire to create new forms suitable to the piano. Not only did he evolve these forms, but they led him inevitably, so to speak, to the invention of aesthetic structures never before utilized, which constitute types of perfection that no one after him has yet known how to employ.

If he revived the old form of a Prelude preceding a Fugue so generally used in the eighteenth century, as illustrated in the works of J. S. Bach, it is to interpose between these two essential elements a Chorale — an art form of a totally different origin, but which is so indispensable in his structure to the other two parts that it can no more be separated from them than the keystone can be removed from the arch. Likewise, the Prelude, Aria and Finale, which, though it derives both from the ancient instrumental Suite and the Sonata, is nevertheless an entirely novel form in music.

Lastly, the Variation — not at all the variation that embroiders a theme, such as Mozart and his imitators wrote by the hundreds, but the variation of broad development, invented by Bach, and raised by Beethoven in his later manner to the height of a fundamental art-form — the variation was chosen by César Franck as the basis for two other works in which the piano bears a prominent part, though in connection with the orchestra. I speak of *Les Djinns* and the *Variations symphoniques*.

ARRIVONS maintenant à l'œuvre de piano de César Franck.

Chose curieuse et qui ne se présente, à ma connaissance, chez aucun autre musicien que chez celui qui nous occupe, les compositions de ce genre se trouvent réparties aux deux extrémités de sa carrière. C'est ainsi que toute la production des cinq premières années, de 1842 à 1846, ne consiste guère, à part les quatre trios, qu'en pièces pour piano seul, puis, tout à coup, Franck cesse complètement et durant près de quarante ans, d'écrire pour l'instrument cher aux Liszt et aux Chopin, et ce n'est qu'à la fin de sa vie, dans la période de cinq années qui s'étend de 1885 jusqu'à sa mort, qu'il est hanté par le désir de créer de nouvelles formules applicables au clavier à percussion, et non seulement il trouve ces formules mais elles l'amènent pour ainsi dire fatalement à la découverte de formes esthétiques non encore usitées et constituant des types parfaits dont on n'a point encore su, après lui, tirer parti.

S'il fait revivre l'ancienne forme du *prélude* précédant une *fugue*, très répandue au XVIIIe siècle et illustrée par S. Bach, c'est pour intercaler entre ces deux éléments essentiels un *choral*, composition provenant originairement d'un ordre d'idées tout opposé, mais qui, cependant, dans cette œuvre, est tellement indispensable aux autres pièces qu'elle ne saurait en être séparée et que celles-ci sembleraient sans cette clef de voûte, comme un monument incomplet. De même, le *Prélude, aria et final*, qui procède à la fois de l'ancienne *suite instrumentale* et de la *sonate*, est encore une composition de forme absolument nouvelle.

Enfin, la forme *variation*, et non point la variation calquée sur le thème comme Mozart et ses imitateurs en ont produit par centaines, mais la grande variation amplificatrice, créée par Bach et élevée par Beethoven, en sa troisième manière, jusqu'à la hauteur d'un principe esthétique, la forme *variation* fut pour César Franck le prétexte de deux autres œuvres dans lesquelles, bien qu'associé à l'orchestre, le piano prend une grande part, je veux parler des *Djinns* et des *Variations symphoniques*.

Toward the end of his life he amused himself by making arrangements for four hands or for two pianos of some of his orchestral works; not to speak of his choral compositions, sacred and secular, *Ruth, Le Rédemption, Rebecca, Les Béatitudes,* for which he endeavored himself to make the piano scores. In all these varied transcriptions one can always recognize his care for the logical, harmonic and (so to speak) architectural forms—a care which he demonstrated all his life, even in his writing for piano.

The pieces which are comprised in the present collection give a virtually complete idea of Franck's quality as a piano composer. If we have been obliged to select from his early works only those which seemed to us to indicate most faithfully that somewhat neglected period in his life, laying aside those which were of slight interest, we have included all the piano compositions of his later years, together with his original transcriptions of symphonic music: excepting, however, those arrangements for two pianos which were outside the scope of these volumes.

From the early works we have chosen the *Eglogue* (1842), the *Grand Caprice* (1843) and the *Ballade* (1844), preceding them with César Franck's three first efforts in composition, written at the age of thirteen years. These have not been published hitherto, and we are indebted for them to the kindness of M. Ch. Malherbe, the erudite librarian of the Académie de Musique.

The mature style of the master is shown in his two most important piano works, the *Prelude, Chorale and Fugue* (1884), and the *Prelude, Aria and Finale* (1886), and also in two short pieces, *Plaintes d'une poupée* (1865) and *Danse lente* (1885), written for special occasions. Though the latter are simple in style and technique, they show none the less the unmistakable stamp of Franckian melody.

Vers la fin de sa vie, il s'amusa à établir des arrangements pour quatre mains ou deux pianos de certaines de ces œuvres pour orchestre, sans parler de ses oratorios sacrés ou profanes, *Ruth, Rédemption, Rébecca,* les *Béatitudes, Psyché,* dont il tint à faire lui-même les réductions. Dans toutes ces diverses transcriptions on reconnaît toujours son souci des formes logiques, harmonieuses et pour ainsi dire architecturales qu'il employa toute sa vie même dans son écriture pour piano.

Les pièces qui font l'objet de la présente publication peuvent donner une idée tout à fait complète du talent de Franck comme compositeur pour piano. Si nous avons dû choisir dans les œuvres de sa jeunesse celles qui nous paraissaient les plus propres à faire connaître cette époque un peu ignorée de la vie du maître, en laissant de côté celles qui ne nous semblaient offrir qu'un médiocre intérêt, nous avons tenu à présenter intégralement toute la production pour piano seul des dernières années, y compris les arrangements *originaux* des pièces symphoniques, mais en exceptant toutefois les transcriptions pour deux pianos qui ne pouvaient entrer dans les conditions de la publication.

De la première manière, nous donnons l'*Eglogue* (1842), le *Grand caprice* (1843) et la *Ballade* (1844) que nous faisons précéder des trois premiers essais de composition de César Franck, piécettes inédites qu'il écrivit à l'âge de treize ans et dont nous devons la communication à l'obligeance de M. Ch. Malherbe, l'érudit bibliothécaire de l'Académie de musique.

Le style définitif du maître sera représenté par ses deux œuvres capitales, le *Prélude, choral et fugue* (1884) et le *Prélude, aria et final* (1886), et aussi par deux petites pièces, les *Plaintes d'une poupée* (1865) et la *Danse lente* (1885), compositions écrites pour des circonstances spéciales mais qui, pour être d'une compréhension et d'une exécution faciles, n'en offrent pas moins le cachet indéniable de la mélodie franckiste.

I. The Three Earliest Pieces for the Piano. (Unpublished.)

These three little pieces in song-form are found at the end of the "Cahier des études de contrepoint de César Auguste Franck, de Liège," a book written with exquisite neatness, which contains all his counterpoint exercises worked under Reicha's instruction from 1835 to 1836. Following numerous efforts in melody-writing upon themes given by the teacher, there appears toward the last pages this title, written with a triumphant flourish, "Chants de moi, réalisés," at the top of three little melodies in A minor, C major and B minor, the latter already showing individuality. These are the first original compositions written by the composer of the Quartet in D. At the end of the exercise book is mentioned in a naïve manner the death of the teacher, Antoine Reicha, who had thus far guided the first steps of the master.

II. Eglogue (*Hirten Gedicht*), Op. 3
"*composée pour le piano par César Auguste Franck, de Liège, et dédiée à Madame la Baronne de Chabannes,*" *1842.* (Published by Schlésinger.)

An introduction of twenty-six measures in E♭ major, which is suggestive of certain themes in *Ruth*, leads to a long exposition, also in E♭, which gives place (especially in the second part) to some novel experiments in piano technique —evidences of which we find even in his later compositions.

Franck, like Weber, had a very large hand; consequently he frequently wrote chords which demand a very wide stretch between the thumb and fifth finger. By reason of these stretches there are many passages which are extremely difficult to write on two staves, particularly so when, as in this *Eglogue*, there is an added melody divided between the two hands. At that time Liszt alone was bold enough to employ three staves in the writing of piano music, and beginners, like the young César Auguste, would never have dared permit themselves such a liberty. Nevertheless, how much clearer for the reader would the exposition of the second theme have appeared if noted thus:

1: Les trois premières pièces pour piano (inédites).

Ces trois courtes pièces de forme *lied* se trouvent à la fin du "*Cahier des études de contrepoint de César Auguste Franck, de Liège,*" cahier extrêmement soigné comme graphique, qui contient tous les exercices de contrepoint faits sous la direction de Reicha, de 1835 à 1836. Après de nombreux essais de construction mélodique sur des thèmes donnés par le professeur, apparaît vers les dernières pages ce titre, triomphalement calligraphié: "*Chants de moi, réalisés,*" en tête de trois petites mélodies en *la mineur, ut majeur* et *si mineur,* celle-ci déjà presque personnelle; ce sont donc bien les premières compositions authentiques écrites par l'auteur du *Quatuor en ré.* A la fin du cahier, est mentionnée, en termes ingénus, la mort du professeur qui avait, jusque là, guidé les premiers pas du maître, Antoine Reicha.

2: Eglogue (*Hirten Gedicht*), op. 3
"*composée pour le piano par César Auguste Franck, de Liège, et dédiée à Madame la Baronne de Chabannes.*" 1842 (Schlésinger, éditeur).

Une introduction de vingt-six mesures en *mi* ♭ *majeur*, dont la mélodie fait pressentir certains thèmes de *Ruth*, conduit à une longue exposition, également en *mi* ♭, qui donne lieu, surtout dans sa seconde partie, à des recherches d'écriture instrumentale vraiment curieuses et dont on retrouve des traces jusque dans les dernières œuvres.

Franck, comme Weber, avait les mains fort grandes; il lui arrive, en conséquence, fréquemment, d'écrire des accords qui exigent un extrême écartement entre le pouce et le cinquième doigt; certains passages, en raison de ces écarts, sont donc assez difficiles à noter sur deux portées, surtout lorsque, comme dans cette églogue, s'y superpose une mélodie à diviser entre les deux mains. A cette époque, Liszt seul avait osé employer l'écriture de piano sur trois portées et les commençants comme le jeune César Auguste, n'étaient point autorisés à se permettre cette licence; et cependant, combien plus claire eut apparu aux yeux du lecteur la fréquente expo-

After a short development of the theme of the introduction and of the above melody a thunderstorm interrupts, which brings back the second theme, first in C minor, then in C major; and finally the same part reappears for conclusion in its original form and tonality.

In this piece Franck, who later became one of the most expert technicians that ever lived, seems to have been afraid to modulate, and the tonality of E♭ grows much too insistent.

III. PREMIER GRAND CAPRICE, Op. 5

"*composée pour le piano par César Auguste Franck, de Liège, et dédié à Madame Cordier,*" *1843*. (Published by Henri Lemoine, Paris.)

Like the preceding piece, this Caprice is divided into three parts, commencing with the double exposition of two themes which are both announced in the key of G♭ major, but one in $\frac{4}{4}$ and the other in $\frac{6}{8}$ time. It proceeds with a lively movement in F♯ minor; then follows a return of the two opening themes, developed as in the first part, and a concluding section brings the piece to an end. Though musicianly enough, this Caprice addresses itself chiefly to lovers of virtuosity.

IV. BALLADE, Op. 9. 1844.

Though this piece was evidently printed, it is impossible to procure it of any of the publishing firms which succeeded those existing in 1844; nor is there any copyright record of it either with the Bibliothèque Nationale or the Conservatoire. We have had to obtain permission, therefore, to make a copy of the original manuscript.

It is written in the key of B major, for which

sition du second thème, si elle eut été notée ainsi :

Après un court développement du thème de l'introduction et de la mélodie ci-dessus, survient un *orage* (allegro en *ut mineur*) qui ramène le second thème en *ut mineur*, puis *majeur*, et enfin, ce même élément reparaît pour conclure dans sa forme et sa tonalité primitives.

Dans ce morceau, Franck, qui fut depuis l'un des plus puissants manieurs de *tons*, semble ne pas oser moduler et, véritablement, la tonalité de *mi* ♭ paraît quelque peu abusive.

3: PREMIER GRAND CAPRICE, op. 5

"*composé pour le piano par César Auguste Francke, de Liège, et dédié à Madame Cordier.*" 1843 (Henry Lemoine, éditeur).

Comme la pièce précédente, ce caprice est coupé en trois parties ; commençant par une double exposition de deux thèmes qui sont tous deux présentés dans la tonalité de *sol* ♭ *majeur*, mais l'un à $\frac{4}{4}$, l'autre à $\frac{6}{8}$, il continue par un mouvement vif en *fa* ♯ *mineur*, après quoi la réexposition des deux idées se fait comme dans la partie initiale, puis, une phrase conclusive vient terminer la pièce qui, bien que suffisamment musicale, s'adresse plus particulièrement aux amateurs de virtuosité.

4: PREMIÈRE BALLADE, op. 9. 1844.

Cette pièce dut évidemment être éditée, mais il est actuellement impossible de se la procurer dans aucune des maisons d'édition qui succédèrent à celles existant en 1844, le dépôt légal n'en fut fait ni à la Bibliothèque nationale ni à celle du Conservatoire et nous avons dû avoir recours au

"le père Franck" had a special affection, and which was always conducive to his inspiration from the first trios to the sublime Adagio in the string quartet. The Ballade commences, after an introduction of forty-nine measures, with a series of developments in the same tonality of a theme whose personal traits are already marked —traits of which one finds the essential character much later in the works of the composer's maturity. There follows an Allegro in B minor, very pianistic in its idiom, which modulates prudently only to the dominant, and which brings a return of the opening theme for the third section, but ornamented with torrents of sixteenthnotes after the fashion then prevailing.

It is interesting to observe that all the early piano compositions of the master are cast in the same mould: an allegro interposed between two expositions of an identical theme, the whole preceded by a short introduction. They likewise exhibit a conspicuously uniform tonality, owing to the almost complete absence of modulation, and they seem to have virtuosity for their sole objective. However, on closer examination, one finds frequently, as I have said, an inspiration derived from the great works of the past; and the desire to exploit a brilliant pianistic style often yields to the search for ideas which are purely musical.

Evidently Franck was at that time under pressure from his father to compose rapidly such pieces as would sell readily, and he wisely adhered to a simple plan that was easy of comprehension.

We shall see him in his second period of writing for the piano in full possession of his incomparable gift for construction.

V. THE DOLL'S LAMENT
"*dédiée à son élève Mlle. Gabrielle Oeschger*," *1865*. (Unpublished.)

It was for a young girl of twelve years, to whom he gave piano lessons, that Franck composed this *bluette*, which, in its two-voiced writing, recalls the melodic simplicity of the charming Inventions by J. S. Bach.

manuscrit original dont il nous a été permis de prendre copie.

Elle est écrite dans ce ton de *si majeur* que le père Franck affectionnait particulièrement et qui fut toujours favorable à son inspiration, depuis les premiers trios jusqu'au sublime adagio du *Quatuor à cordes*.

La *Ballade* commence, après une introduction de quarante-neuf mesures, par plusieurs expositions successives et monotonales d'un thème déjà personnel et dont on retrouve plus tard les contours essentiels dans les œuvres de maturité; puis, vient un allegro en *si mineur* dont les formes, très pianistiques, ne tendent que vers une prudente inflexion au ton de la dominante et qui ramène en troisième lieu une ré-exposition du thème primitif, agrémenté de batteries en doubles croches selon la formule alors répandue.

Il est assez intéressant de constater que toutes les premières compositions pour piano du maître sont coulées dans le même moule: un allegro encadré entre deux expositions d'un même thème, le tout précédé d'une courte introduction. Elles présentent, au surplus, une assez notable monotonie par l'absence presque complète de modulations et semblent avoir pour unique but la virtuosité, mais, en les examinant de près, on y retrouve assez fréquemment, ainsi que je l'ai dit, l'inspiration des grandes œuvres postérieures, et le souci du brillant de l'écriture instrumentale n'est point tel qu'il ne cède souvent le pas à la recherche des formes purement musicales.

Evidemment, Franck, à cette époque, pressé par son père de produire rapidement des œuvres *de vente*, s'en tient prudemment à l'exécution d'un plan simple et facile à réaliser.

Nous allons le voir, dans la seconde période de sa production pour piano, en pleine possession de son talent de constructeur hors ligne.

5: LES PLAINTES D'UNE POUPÉE (œuvre inédite)
"*dédiée à son élève Melle Gabrielle Oeschger*." 1865.

C'est pour une jeune fille de douze ans à laquelle il donnait des leçons de piano, que Franck composa cette bluette dont l'écriture à deux parties

VI. DANSE LENTE, in F minor. 1885. (Unpublished.)

In 1885 and 1886 the journal "Le Gaulois" published two music albums, for which it solicited contributions of unpublished pieces from contemporary composers of varying excellence. The second of these albums consisted of a collection of dances for piano. It was at the request of M. L. de Fourcaud, who was in charge of editing these collections, that Franck wrote this easy little piece, so charming and so characteristic. To-day it is almost impossible to find it, for the album of "Le Gaulois" for 1886 printed but a small edition, which was entirely exhausted; and it was never deposited either with the Bibliothèque Nationale or with the Library of the Conservatoire.

VII. PRELUDE, CHORAL AND FUGUE, FOR PIANO "*dédié à Mademoiselle Marie Poitevin*" (Madame Georges Haine), *1884–85*. (Published in Collection Litolff, Enoch et Cie.)

When this beautiful work appeared a long period had elapsed, during which composers had neglected serious piano composition.

After the avalanche of fantasias and the plethora of concertos which marked the first half of the nineteenth century, it seemed as though the instrument which had inherited the great works written for the clavichord by Bach, Haydn and Mozart, and through the sonatas of Beethoven had won its patent of nobility, was destined, musically speaking, to a sterile decadence. For though great artists — specialists of the keyboard — had brought manual dexterity and ingenuity to the point of perfection; though Schumann, in order to express his thought through genial little pieces, evolved a style rich in novel colorings and intimate tonal gradations; though Liszt, demolishing with a stroke of his wing the scaffolding of classic technique, endowed the instrument with hitherto undreamed of combinations, and gave to virtuosity a final flight; still there had been no genius who had brought actually new art material to add to the Beethovenian structure.

The sonata form, that splendid and logical outcome of the symphonic development begun

rappelle en sa simplicité mélodique les plus charmantes *inventions* de J. S. Bach.

6: DANSE LENTE *en fa mineur* (œuvre inédite) 1885.

En 1885 et 1886, le journal le *Gaulois* publia deux albums musicaux pour lesquels il demanda à des compositeurs contemporains, d'inégale valeur, d'écrire une œuvre inédite. Le second de ces albums était un recueil de danses pour piano. Ce fut à l'instigation de M. L. de Fourcaud, chargé de la mise au point de ces albums, que Franck écrivit cette charmante petite pièce facile et bien personnelle qui est, à l'heure actuelle, devenue presque introuvable car l'album du *Gaulois* de 1886, tiré à un très petit nombre d'exemplaires, est entièrement épuisé et qu'il n'a été déposé ni à la bibliothèque du Conservatoire, ni à la Bibliothèque nationale.

7: PRÉLUDE, CHORAL ET FUGUE *pour piano* "*dédié à Mademoiselle Marie Poitevin*" (*M*ᵐᵉ *Georges Hainl*), 1884–85 (Collection Litolff, Enoch et Cⁱᵉ, éditeurs).

Lorsque parut cette belle œuvre, il y avait longtemps déjà que les compositeurs négligeaient d'écrire sérieusement pour le piano.

Après l'avalanche de fantaisies et la pléthore de concertos qui caractérisèrent la production de la première moitié du XIXᵉ siècle, il semblait que l'instrument héritier des chefs-d'œuvre écrits pour le clavecin par les Bach, Haydn et Mozart, et qui avait, de par les sonates de Beethoven, conquis ses titres de noblesse, fut voué, musicalement parlant, à une inféconde décadence. Si de grands artistes, spécialistes du piano, avaient apporté d'ingénieux perfectionnements à sa technique manuelle, si un Schumann trouvait pour exprimer sa pensée en de géniales piécettes, une écriture riche en teintes nouvelles et en intimes sonorités, si un Liszt, démolissant d'un coup d'aile l'échafaudage du *pianisme* classique, dotait l'instrument de combinaisons jusqu'alors insoupçonnées et donnait à la virtuosité un décisif essor, aucun maître n'avait toutefois apporté de nouveaux *matériaux d'art* à l'édifice beethovénien.

in the seventeenth century, had progressed not at all beyond the giant strides made by Beethoven in Op. 106 and Op. 110, and in the quartets, Op. 127 and Op. 132. Whether through indifference, timidity or a lack of architectural skill, neither Mendelssohn, Schubert nor Weber, Schumann, Chopin, Liszt, nor even Brahms, had dared to make any innovations in that form of composition. There is nothing more awkward than the sonatas of Schumann and of Chopin, unless it be those of Grieg; and, in short, if the technique and the material side of piano composition had become absolutely transcendental, the musical content itself had strongly degenerated, and it is a truism that all forms which do not exhibit any progress end in atrophy and ultimate disappearance.

The important movement started in France by the Société Nationale de Musique had brought forth but a few interesting works for piano alone, as its efforts were directed mainly toward orchestra and chamber music.

Thus it was that César Franck, struck by the poverty of serious compositions in this genre, devoted himself with a zeal that was wholly youthful, in spite of his sixty years, to the search for an adaptation of time-honored forms to the modern piano technique — a search which resulted in some noteworthy modifications of those forms.

Having originally the intention of writing a prelude and fugue for piano after the style of those by Bach, the idea soon occurred to him of binding these two parts together by a chorale, and thus creating an entirely original form in which nothing should be left haphazard but wherein all the material without exception should contribute harmoniously to the beauty and solidarity of the entire structure.

The Prelude is cast in the historic mould of the classical Suite. A simple theme is announced in the tonic, then in the dominant, and the piece concludes with a phrase that completes the exposition of the theme.

The Chorale is in three periods, shifting from E♭ minor to C minor, and presents two distinct elements: a beautifully expressive phrase which presages the subject of the Fugue, and the Cho-

La *forme sonate*, cette admirable et logique résultante de l'évolution symphonique commencée au XVIIᵉ siècle, n'avait point progressé depuis les pas de géant des œuvres 106 et 110, des quatuors, op. 127 et 132; soit insouciance, timidité ou manque d'habileté dans le métier de constructeur, ni Mendelssohn, ni Schubert, ni Weber, pas plus que Schumann, Chopin, Liszt et Brahms lui-même, n'avaient osé innover dans ce genre de composition; rien de plus maladroit que les sonates de Schumann et de Chopin si ce n'est peut-être celles de Grieg; bref, si la technique et l'écriture matérielle du piano étaient devenues absolument transcendantes, la musique destinée à l'instrument *seul* avait fortement dégénéré; il est naturel en effet que toute forme qui ne progresse point finisse par s'atrophier et disparaître.

L'important mouvement créé en France par la Société nationale de musique n'avait produit que de rares pièces intéressantes pour piano seul, toute son action se portant vers l'orchestre et la musique de chambre.

C'est alors que César Franck, frappé de la pénurie d'œuvres sérieuses en ce genre, s'attacha avec une ardeur toute juvénile, malgré ses soixante ans, à chercher l'adaptation des anciennes formes traditionnelles à la nouvelle technique du piano, recherche qui aboutit à d'assez notables modifications de ces formes.

Ayant primitivement l'intention d'écrire un *prélude et fugue* pour piano dans le style de ceux de Bach, il accueillit bientôt l'idée de relier ces deux pièces par un Choral et de faire ainsi une création toute personnelle où rien n'est cependant laissé au hasard mais dans laquelle tous les matériaux sans en excepter aucun concourent harmonieusement à la beauté et à la solidité du monument.

Le *prélude* reste dans le moule classique du prélude de la *suite*. Son thème unique s'expose à la tonique puis à la dominante et se termine par une phrase qui complète le sens du thème.

Le *choral*, en trois périodes, oscillant de *mi* ♭ *mineur* à *ut mineur*, présente deux éléments distincts: une belle phrase expressive présageant le futur sujet de la fugue et le choral proprement

rale proper, whose three melodic sections are superposed with incomparable majesty.

After an interlude which leads us from E♭ minor to B minor (the principal key), the Fugue unfolds its successive sections which are subjected to development, and then the design and the rhythm of the concluding phrase of the Prelude are brought back. Soon the rhythm alone persists, to accompany a restatement of the theme of the Chorale; later the subject of the Fugue itself enters in the principal key, in such fashion that the three chief components of the entire work are combined in a superb and triumphant peroration.

The most important of the musical themes, and the one which binds together the various portions of the work and gives it such admirable unity, is without question the Subject of the Fugue. This is first encountered in the second page of the Prelude in a form which is truly a trifle rudimentary, but none the less entirely recognizable.

It is defined more clearly in the phrase leading up to the Chorale:

Finally, after its regular development in the first entry of the Fugue:

In the peroration it is brought back thus, combined with the other thematic material:

dit dont les trois fragments mélodiques s'imposent avec une majesté incomparable.

Après un intermède qui nous ramène de *mi ♭ mineur* à *si mineur*, ton principal, la *fugue* vient dérouler ses successives expositions après le développement desquelles sont ramenés le dessin et le rythme de la phrase complémentaire du prélude; bientôt le rythme seul persiste, accompagnant une reprise très mouvementée du thème du choral, peu après, le sujet de la fugue entre lui-même au ton principal, en sorte que les trois éléments principaux de l'œuvre se trouvent réunis en une admirable et triomphante péroraison.

L'idée musicale la plus importante, celle qui relie entr'elles les diverses parties de l'œuvre et leur donne cette admirable cohésion est, sans contredit, le sujet de la fugue. On le rencontre dès la deuxième page du prélude sous une forme, à la vérité, un peu rudimentaire mais néanmoins fort reconnaissable:

il se précise davantage dans la phrase qui prépare l'avènement du choral:

enfin, après son exposition régulière dans la première entrée de la fugue:

la péroraison le ramène ainsi combiné avec les autres éléments:

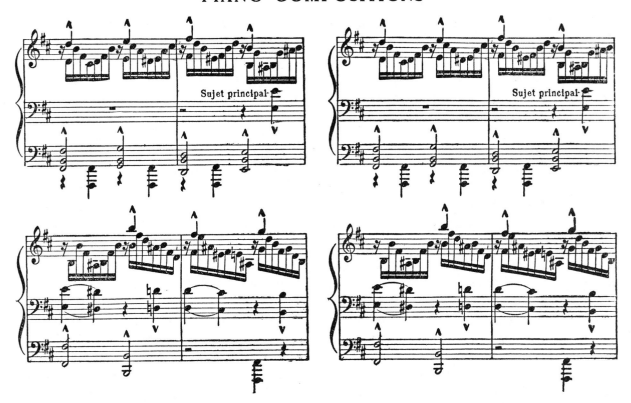

It is obvious that in the interpretation of this brilliant climax it is the Subject of the Fugue which should be brought into high relief by the performer; for it may be said that it is the key to the entire work, appearing throughout at regular intervals, only to rise at the close to the fullness of its victorious stature.

VIII. Prelude, Aria and Finale, for the Piano

"*dédié à Madame Bordes-Pêne,*" *1885–86.* (Published by Hamelle.)

Very different from the work analyzed above is the construction of this one, which brings to the sonata form the same elements of growth as the preceding composition supplied to the prelude with fugue.

In the work now being considered the Prelude has for its theme an extended section, consisting of four periods, an astounding and extended flight of inspiration. It is repeated in the relative key toward the middle of the composition and reappears in E major (the principal key) at the end, but slightly modified.

Il est donc évident que, dans l'interprétation de cette conclusion étincelante, c'est le sujet de la fugue qui doit être mis en lumière par l'exécutant, puisqu'il est, pour ainsi dire, la clef de l'œuvre entière au cours de laquelle il paraît à intervalles réguliers pour ne prendre qu'en terminant sa victorieuse personnalité.

8: Prélude, Aria et Final, *pour piano*

"*dédié à Madame Bordes-Pêne.*" 1885–86 (Hamelle, éditeur).

Très différente de celle que nous venons d'examiner est la construction de cette œuvre qui apporte à la *forme sonate* les mêmes éléments de rénovation que la précédente apportait au *prélude et fugue.*

Le prélude de celle-ci a pour thème une longue phrase en quatre périodes d'une inspiration étonnamment soutenue, elle se répète au ton relatif vers le milieu de la pièce et reparaît en *mi majeur,* ton principal, à la fin, mais légèrement modifiée.

On reconnaît ici la *forme andante* de *sonate* adaptée à un prélude de *suite.* L'aria qui est au

One may recognize here the Andante from the sonata adapted to the Prelude of a suite. The Aria, which is on the contrary borrowed from the suite-form where it functions like the Andante in a sonata, discloses and repeats a noble and calm melody which moves from Ab major to Ab minor, enclosed between a short introduction and a concluding passage which serves to establish the succeeding Finale.

The last number presents all the framework of the sonata form, with this exception, that the principal tonality does not make its appearance until the reëxposition of the second theme. Then it is maintained without modulation until the close. The effect of radiant light produced by the return of this tonality is as though it had laboriously emerged a conqueror through a long series of tonal gradations, marvellously managed.

After the classic development of the themes, the Aria makes a quiet reappearance, without its enfolding figuration, in Db major. Then, as a counterpart, the beautiful melody of the Prelude instals itself vigorously in the principal key, after a fresh development of the two themes, to blend in colors expressively softened with the elements of the Aria—finally to close gently in a sort of evaporation of the melody which seems to wing forth into space.

It is difficult to decide which of these two works is the more beautiful; but it may be unhesitatingly affirmed that they have given a new flight to piano composition, which was degenerating into a futile virtuosity.

I do not consider it necessary to go into detail concerning the transcriptions for four hands of *Les Eolides*, *Le Chasseur maudit*, and the Symphony in D minor, merely remarking upon the careful and logical manner of writing therein disclosed. I wish to say, however, in completing this study of the piano compositions of my master, César Franck, that to interpret them worthily it will not suffice to possess an easy mechanism and a flawless technique. That which is required at the outset is to divest one's self of all vanity, so that one is willing **to place music**

contraire coupée dans la *forme suite* tout en faisant fonction d'andante de sonate, expose par deux fois une noble et tranquille mélodie qui se meut de *la ♭ majeur* à *la ♭ mineur*, encadrée entre une introduction courte et une conclusion qui servira à établir l'équilibre du final.

Quant à la dernière pièce, elle présente toute l'ossature de la *forme sonate*, avec cette circonstance exceptionelle que la tonalité principale n'y fait son apparition que lors de la réexposition du deuxième thème pour se maintenir sans moduler jusqu'à la fin. L'effet de radieuse lumière produit par le retour de cette tonalité provient de ce qu'elle a été péniblement conquise par une gradation tonale merveilleusement nuancée.

Après le développement classique des idées, l'*aria* reparaît, calme, malgré son enveloppement mouvementé, en *ré ♭ majeur*, puis, comme contrepartie, c'est la belle mélodie du *prélude* qui, après la réexposition des deux thèmes, s'installe vigoureusement dans la tonalité principale pour se mêler en teintes expressivement dégradées aux éléments de l'*aria* et terminer doucement par une sorte d'évaporation de la mélodie qui semble fuir à travers l'espace.

Il est difficile de décider laquelle de ces deux belles œuvres est la plus géniale, mais ce que l'on peut affirmer à coup sûr, c'est qu'elles ont donné un nouvel essor à la littérature du piano qui allait s'abâtardissant dans le virtuosisme et la futilité.

Je ne crois pas utile d'entrer dans des détails analytiques au sujet des transcriptions à quatre mains des *Eolides*, du *Chasseur maudit* et de la *Symphonie en ré*, je ferai seulement remarquer combien l'écriture en est toujours logique et soignée, mais ce que je tiens à dire en terminant cette étude sur l'œuvre de piano de mon maître César Franck, c'est que, pour l'interpréter dignement, il ne suffit point de posséder un mécanisme habile, une impeccable technique, mais qu'il est en outre indispensable d'être dénué de toute vanité puisqu'il s'agit de faire passer la *musique* avant l'effet personnel, et surtout d'être

itself before personal exploitation; and above all to be endowed with the three qualities which alone can lift the real artist above the mere virtuoso: Faith, enthusiasm and sincerity.

doué des trois qualités qui, seules, peuvent élever l'*artiste* véritable au dessus du *virtuose*—la foi, l'enthousiasme et la sincérité.

Translated by
CHARLES FONTEYN MANNEY

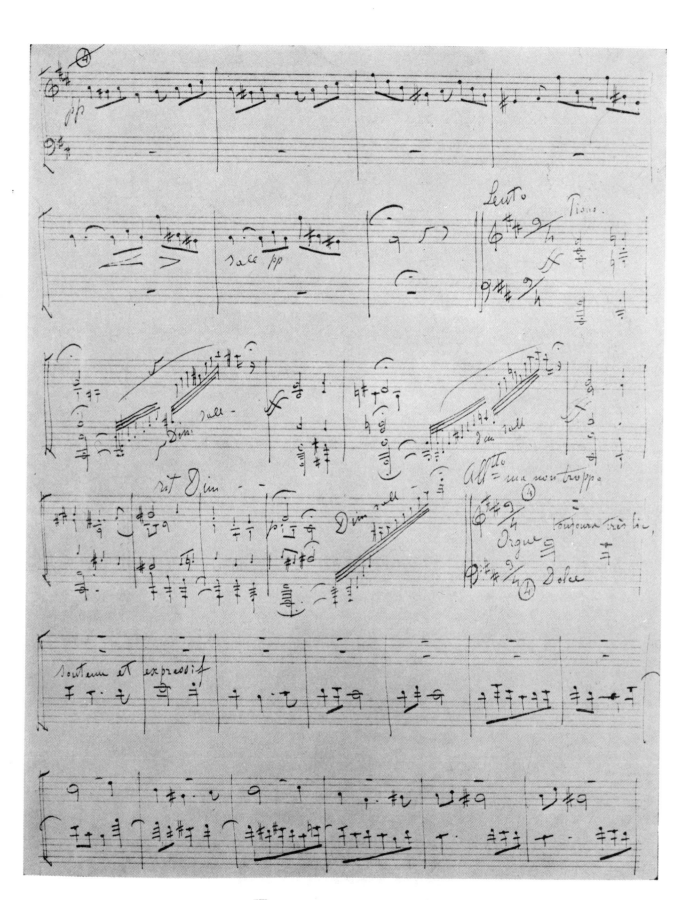

Facsimile of original organ manuscript by César Franck

[Handwritten letter in French — see facsimile]

Facsimile of letter from César Franck to Vincent d'Indy

Monument to César Franck in Paris
(Alfred Lenoir, Sculptor)

SELECTED
PIANO COMPOSITIONS

THE THREE EARLIEST COMPOSITIONS
(LES TROIS PREMIÈRES COMPOSITIONS)
(Composed in 1835)

I

CÉSAR FRANCK

PIANO

These three little piano pieces are taken from Franck's book of exercises in counterpoint and fugue of the year 1835. No I carries these words: *"Chant à moi avec des appogiatures, à accompagner."* These are undoubtedly the first three compositions of César Franck, who was then twelve years and six months old.

II

III

à *Madame la baronne de Chabonnes*

EGLOGUE
(PASTORAL)
(Composed in 1842)

CÉSAR FRANCK, Op. 3

à son élève
Mademoiselle Élodie Cordier Moraquini

PREMIER GRAND CAPRICE

(Composed in 1843)

CÉSAR FRANCK, Op. 5

26

Tempo I. Moderato (♩=96)

dolce tenero

Prestissimo

rall.

a tempo

più f

Non troppo vivo

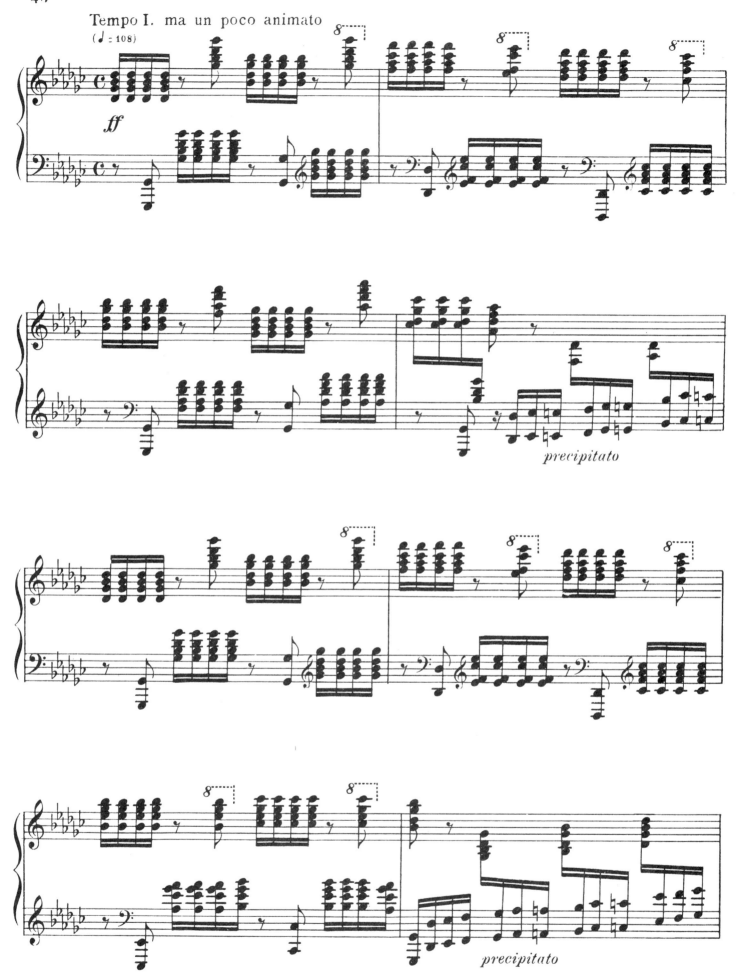

a son éléve
Mademoiselle Athanasie Adour

BALLADE

(Composed in 1844)

CESAR FRANCK, Op.9

Allegro molto (♩=126)

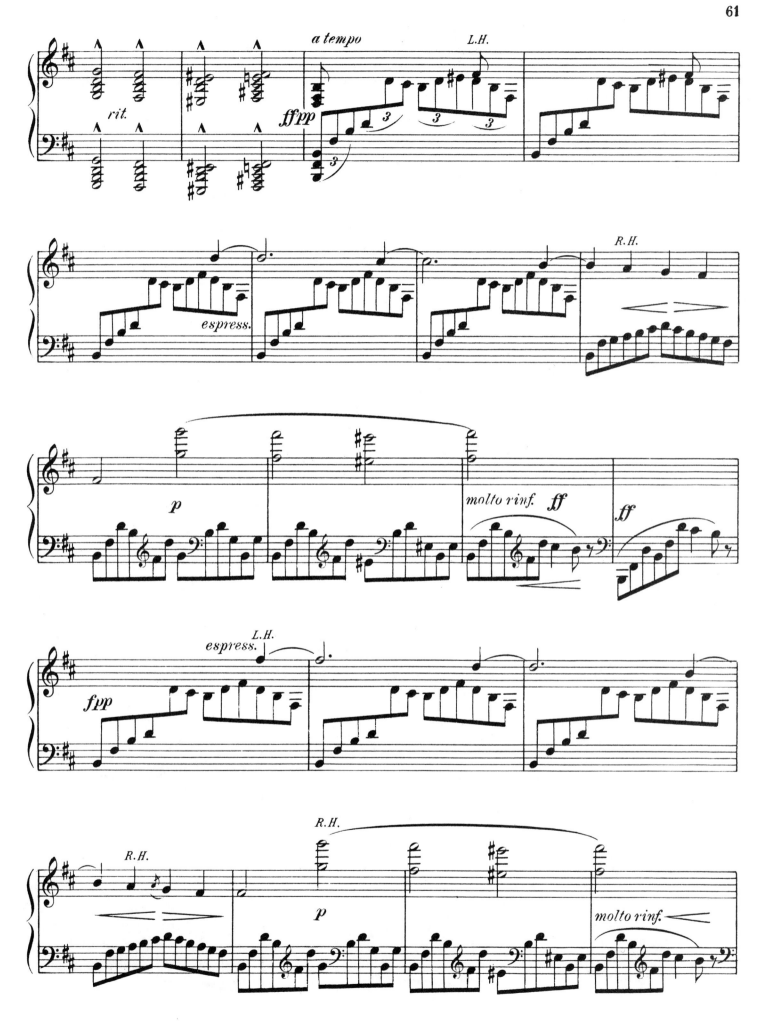

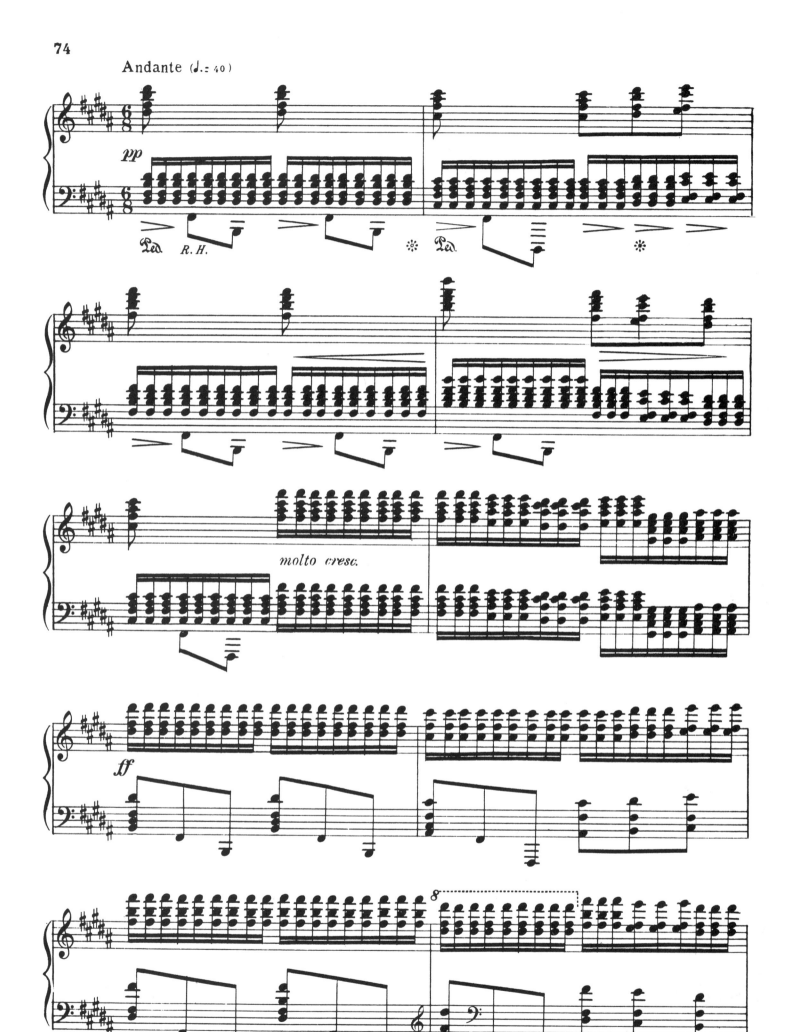

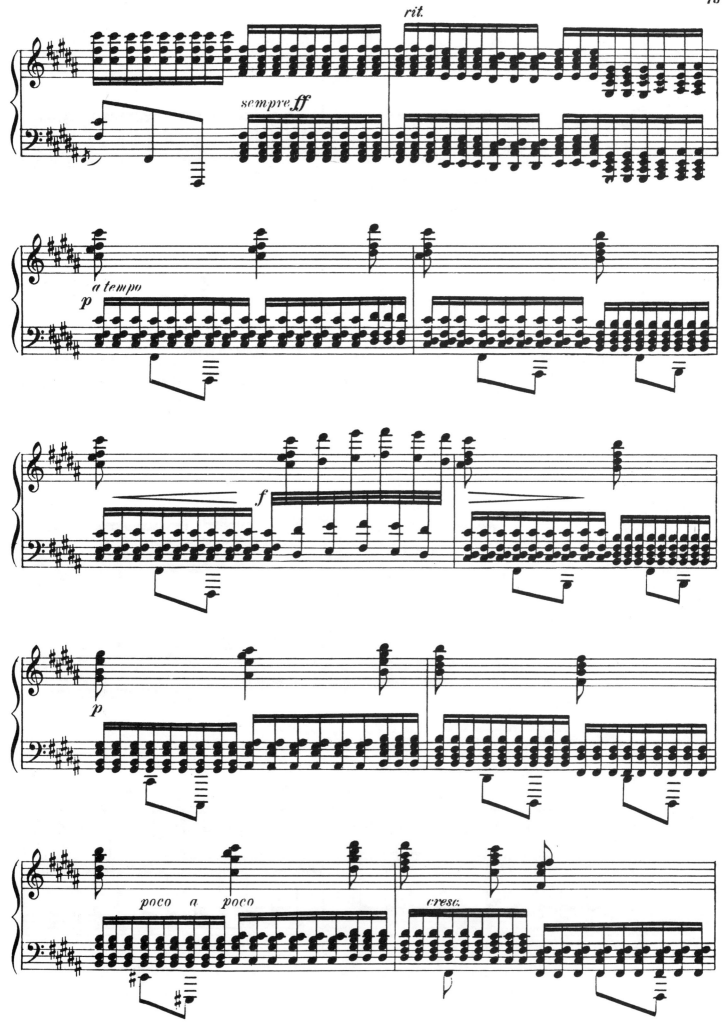

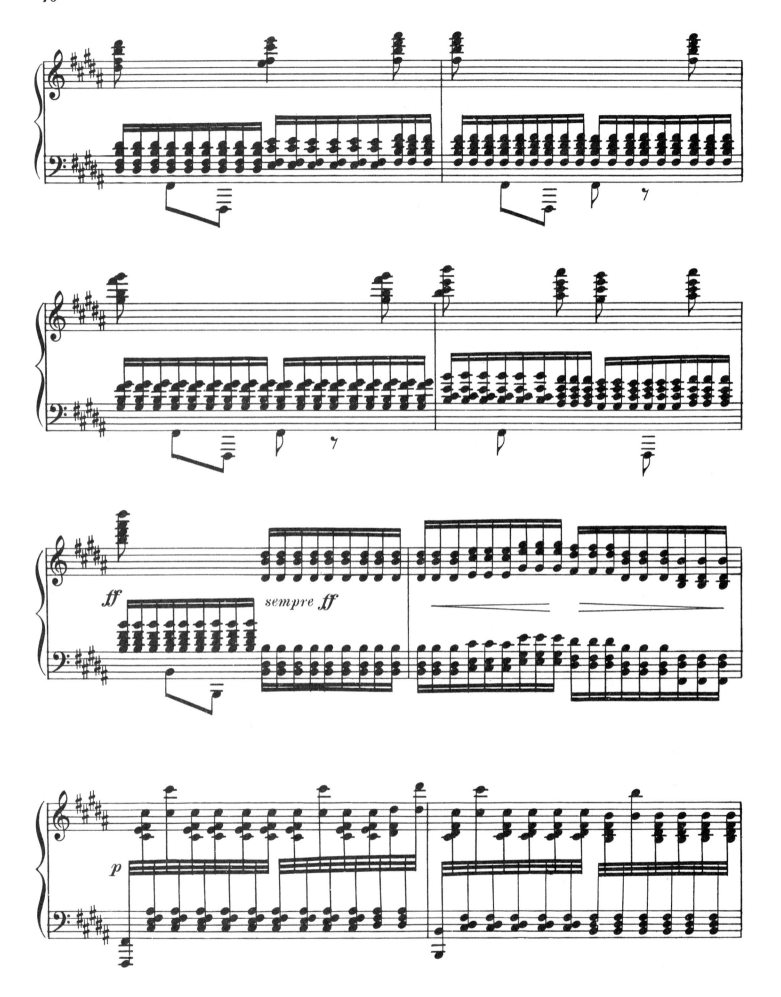

à Mademoiselle Gabrielle Oeschger

THE DOLL'S LAMENT
(LES PLAINTES D'UNE POUPÉE)

(Composed in 1865)

CÉSAR FRANCK

à Mademoiselle Marie Poitevin

PRELUDE, CHORAL AND FUGUE

(Composed in 1884)

CÉSAR FRANCK

PRELUDE
Moderato

PIANO

Choral

Fugue

DANSE LENTE

(Composed in 1885)

CÉSAR FRANCK

PRELUDE, ARIA AND FINALE

(Composed in 1886)

PRELUDE

Allegro moderato e maestoso (♩ = 116)

CÉSAR FRANCK

Poco animato (♩ = 132)

FINALE

Allegro molto ed agitato (♩=88)

Tempo I. (♩=88)

Dover Piano and Keyboard Editions

THE WELL-TEMPERED CLAVIER: Books I and II, Complete, Johann Sebastian Bach. All 48 preludes and fugues in all major and minor keys. Authoritative Bach-Gesellschaft edition. Explanation of ornaments in English, tempo indications, music corrections. 208pp. 9⅜ × 12¼. 24532-2 Pa. **$9.95**

KEYBOARD MUSIC, J. S. Bach. Bach-Gesellschaft edition. For harpsichord, piano, other keyboard instruments. English Suites, French Suites, Six Partitas, Goldberg Variations, Two-Part Inventions, Three-Part Sinfonias. 312pp. 8⅛ × 11. 22360-4 Pa. **$10.95**

ITALIAN CONCERTO, CHROMATIC FANTASIA AND FUGUE AND OTHER WORKS FOR KEYBOARD, Johann Sebastian Bach. Sixteen of Bach's best-known, most-performed and most-recorded works for the keyboard, reproduced from the authoritative Bach-Gesellschaft edition. 112pp. 9 × 12. 25387-2 Pa. **$8.95**

COMPLETE KEYBOARD TRANSCRIPTIONS OF CONCERTOS BY BAROQUE COMPOSERS, Johann Sebastian Bach. Sixteen concertos by Vivaldi, Telemann and others, transcribed for solo keyboard instruments. Bach-Gesellschaft edition. 128pp. 9⅜ × 12¼. 25529-8 Pa. **$8.95**

ORGAN MUSIC, J. S. Bach. Bach-Gesellschaft edition. 93 works. 6 Trio Sonatas, German Organ Mass, Orgelbüchlein, Six Schubler Chorales, 18 Choral Preludes. 357pp. 8⅛ × 11. 22359-0 Pa. **$12.95**

COMPLETE PRELUDES AND FUGUES FOR ORGAN, Johann Sebastian Bach. All 25 of Bach's complete sets of preludes and fugues (i.e. compositions written as pairs), from the authoritative Bach-Gesellschaft edition. 168pp. 8⅞ × 11. 24816-X Pa. **$9.95**

TOCCATAS, FANTASIAS, PASSACAGLIA AND OTHER WORKS FOR ORGAN, J. S. Bach. Over 20 best-loved works including Toccata and Fugue in D minor, BWV 565; Passacaglia and Fugue in C minor, BWV 582, many more. Bach-Gesellschaft edition. 176pp. 9 × 12. 25403-8 Pa. **$9.95**

TWO- AND THREE-PART INVENTIONS, J. S. Bach. Reproduction of original autograph ms. Edited by Eric Simon. 62pp. 8⅛ × 11. 21982-8 Pa. **$7.95**

THE 36 FANTASIAS FOR KEYBOARD, Georg Philipp Telemann. Graceful compositions by 18th-century master. 1923 Breslauer edition. 80pp. 8⅛ × 11. 25365-1 Pa. **$5.95**

GREAT KEYBOARD SONATAS, Carl Philipp Emanuel Bach. Comprehensive two-volume edition contains 51 sonatas by second, most important son of Johann Sebastian Bach. Originality, rich harmony, delicate workmanship. Authoritative French edition. Total of 384pp. 8⅜ × 11¼. Series I 24853-4 Pa. **$9.95**
Series II 24854-2 Pa. **$9.95**

KEYBOARD WORKS/Series One: Ordres I-XIII; Series Two: Ordres XIV-XXVII and Miscellaneous Pieces, François Couperin. Over 200 pieces. Reproduced directly from edition prepared by Johannes Brahms and Friedrich Chrysander. Total of 496pp. 8⅛ × 11.
Series I 25795-9 Pa. **$9.95**
Series II 25796-7 Pa. **$9.95**

KEYBOARD WORKS FOR SOLO INSTRUMENTS, G. F. Handel. 35 neglected works from Handel's vast oeuvre, originally jotted down as improvisations. Includes Eight Great Suites, others. New sequence. 174pp. 9⅜ × 12¼. 24338-9 Pa. **$9.95**

WORKS FOR ORGAN AND KEYBOARD, Jan Pieterszoon Sweelinck. Nearly all of early Dutch composer's difficult-to-find keyboard works. Chorale variations; toccatas, fantasias; variations on secular, dance tunes. Also, incomplete and/or modified works, plus fantasia by John Bull. 272pp. 9 × 12. 24935-2 Pa. **$11.95**

ORGAN WORKS, Dietrich Buxtehude. Complete organ works of extremely influential pre-Bach composer. Toccatas, preludes, chorales, more. Definitive Breitkopf & Härtel edition. 320pp. 8⅜ × 11¼. (Available in U.S. only) 25682-0 Pa. **$12.95**

THE FUGUES ON THE MAGNIFICAT FOR ORGAN OR KEYBOARD, Johann Pachelbel. 94 pieces representative of Pachelbel's magnificent contribution to keyboard composition; can be played on the organ, harpsichord or piano. 100pp. 9 × 12. (Available in U.S. only) 25037-7 Pa. **$7.95**

MY LADY NEVELLS BOOKE OF VIRGINAL MUSIC, William Byrd. 42 compositions in modern notation from 1591 ms. For any keyboard instrument. 245pp. 8⅛ × 11. 22246-2 Pa. **$13.95**

ELIZABETH ROGERS HIR VIRGINALL BOOKE, edited with calligraphy by Charles J. F. Cofone. All 112 pieces from noted 1656 manuscript, most never before published. Composers include Thomas Brewer, William Byrd, Orlando Gibbons, etc. 125pp. 9 × 12. 23138-0 Pa. **$10.95**

THE FITZWILLIAM VIRGINAL BOOK, edited by J. Fuller Maitland, W. B. Squire. Famous early 17th-century collection of keyboard music, 300 works by Morley, Byrd, Bull, Gibbons, etc. Modern notation. Total of 938pp. 8⅜ × 11. Two-vol. set.
21068-5, 21069-3 Pa. **$33.90**

GREAT KEYBOARD SONATAS, Series I and Series II, Domenico Scarlatti. 78 of the most popular sonatas reproduced from the G. Ricordi edition edited by Alessandro Longo. Total of 320pp. 8⅝ × 11¼.
Series I 24996-4 Pa. **$7.95**
Series II 25003-2 Pa. **$8.95**

SONATAS AND FANTASIES FOR THE PIANO, W. A. Mozart, edited by Nathan Broder. Finest, most accurate edition, based on autographs and earliest editions. 19 sonatas, plus Fantasy and Fugue in C, K.394, Fantasy in C Minor, K.396, Fantasy in D Minor, K.397. 352pp. 9 × 12. (Available in U.S. only) 25417-8 Pa. **$16.50**

COMPLETE PIANO SONATAS, Joseph Haydn. 52 sonatas reprinted from authoritative Breitkopf & Härtel edition. Extremely clear and readable; ample space for notes, analysis. 464pp. 9⅜ × 12¼.
24726-0 Pa. **$10.95**
24727-9 Pa. **$10.95**

BAGATELLES, RONDOS AND OTHER SHORTER WORKS FOR PIANO, Ludwig van Beethoven. Most popular and most performed shorter works, including Rondo a capriccio in G and Andante in F. Breitkopf & Härtel edition. 128pp. 9⅜ × 12¼. 25392-9 Pa. **$8.95**

COMPLETE VARIATIONS FOR SOLO PIANO, Ludwig van Beethoven. Contains all 21 sets of Beethoven's piano variations, including the extremely popular *Diabelli Variations, Op. 120*. 240pp. 9⅜ × 12¼. 25188-8 Pa. **$11.95**

COMPLETE PIANO SONATAS, Ludwig van Beethoven. All sonatas in fine Schenker edition, with fingering, analytical material. One of best modern editions. 615pp. 9 × 12. Two-vol. set.
23134-8, 23135-6 Pa. **$23.90**

COMPLETE SONATAS FOR PIANOFORTE SOLO, Franz Schubert. All 15 sonatas. Breitkopf and Härtel edition. 293pp. 9⅜ × 12¼.
22647-6 Pa. **$13.95**

DANCES FOR SOLO PIANO, Franz Schubert. Over 350 waltzes, minuets, landler, ecossaises, other charming, melodic dance compositions reprinted from the authoritative Breitkopf & Härtel edition. 192pp. 9⅜ × 12¼. 26107-7 Pa. **$9.95**

Available from your music dealer or write for ***free*** *Music Catalog to*
Dover Publications, Inc., Dept. MUBI, 31 East 2nd Street, Mineola, N.Y. 11501.

Dover Piano and Keyboard Editions

ORGAN WORKS, César Franck. Composer's best-known works for organ, including Six Pieces, Trois Pieces, and Trois Chorals. Oblong format for easy use at keyboard. Authoritative Durand edition. 208pp. 11⅜ × 8¼. 25517-4 Pa. **$10.95**

IBERIA AND ESPAÑA: Two Complete Works for Solo Piano, Isaac Albeniz. Spanish composer's greatest piano works in authoritative editions. Includes the popular "Tango". 192pp. 9 × 12. 25367-8 Pa. **$10.95**

GOYESCAS, SPANISH DANCES AND OTHER WORKS FOR SOLO PIANO, Enrique Granados. Great Spanish composer's most admired, most performed suites for the piano, in definitive Spanish editions. 176pp. 9 × 12. 25481-X Pa. **$8.95**

SELECTED PIANO COMPOSITIONS, César Franck, edited by Vincent d'Indy. Outstanding selection of influential French composer's piano works, including early pieces and the two masterpieces—Prelude, Choral and Fugue; and Prelude, Aria and Finale. Ten works in all. 138pp. 9 × 12. 23269-7 Pa. **$9.95**

THE COMPLETE PRELUDES AND ETUDES FOR PIANOFORTE SOLO, Alexander Scriabin. All the preludes and études including many perfectly spun miniatures. Edited by K. N. Igumnov and Y. I. Mil'shteyn. 250pp. 9 × 12. 22919-X Pa. **$10.95**

COMPLETE PIANO SONATAS, Alexander Scriabin. All ten of Scriabin's sonatas, reprinted from an authoritative early Russian edition. 256pp. 8⅜ × 11¼. 25850-5 Pa. **$10.95**

COMPLETE PRELUDES AND ETUDES-TABLEAUX, Serge Rachmaninoff. Forty-one of his greatest works for solo piano, including the riveting C minor, G-minor and B-minor preludes, in authoritative editions. 208pp. 8⅜ × 11¼. (Available in U.S. only) 25696-0 Pa. **$10.95**

COMPLETE PIANO SONATAS, Sergei Prokofiev. Definitive Russian edition of nine sonatas (1907–1953), among the most important compositions in the modern piano repertoire. 288pp. 8⅜ × 11¼. (Available in U.S. only) 25689-8 Pa. **$11.95**

GYMNOPÉDIES, GNOSSIENNES AND OTHER WORKS FOR PIANO, Erik Satie. The largest Satie collection of piano works yet published, 17 in all, reprinted from the original French editions. 176pp. 9 × 12. (Not available in France or Germany) 25978-1 Pa. **$8.95**

TWENTY SHORT PIECES FOR PIANO (Sports et Divertissements), Erik Satie. French master's brilliant thumbnail sketches—verbal and musical—of various outdoor sports and amusements. English translations, 20 illustrations. Rare, limited 1925 edition. 48pp. 12 × 8⅞. (Not available in France or Germany) 24365-6 Pa. **$5.95**

COMPLETE PRELUDES, IMPROMPTUS AND VALSES-CAPRICES, Gabriel Fauré. Eighteen elegantly wrought piano works in authoritative editions. Only one-volume collection. 144pp. 9 × 12. (Not available in France or Germany) 25789-4 Pa. **$8.95**

PIANO MUSIC OF BÉLA BARTÓK, Series I, Béla Bartók. New, definitive Archive Edition incorporating composer's corrections. Includes *Funeral March* from *Kossuth, Fourteen Bagatelles,* Bartók's break to modernism. 167pp. 9 × 12. (Available in U.S. only) 24108-4 Pa. **$10.95**

PIANO MUSIC OF BÉLA BARTÓK, Series II, Béla Bartók. Second in the Archie Edition incorporating composer's corrections. 85 short pieces *For Children, Two Elegies, Two Rumanian Dances,* etc. 192pp. 9 × 12. (Available in U.S. only) 24109-2 Pa. **$10.95**

FRENCH PIANO MUSIC, AN ANTHOLOGY, Isidor Phillipp (ed.). 44 complete works, 1670–1905, by Lully, Couperin, Rameau, Alkan, Saint-Saëns, Delibes, Bizet, Godard, many others; favorites, lesser-known examples, but all top quality. 188pp. 9 × 12. (Not available in France or Germany) 23381-2 Pa. **$9.95**

NINETEENTH-CENTURY EUROPEAN PIANO MUSIC: Unfamiliar Masterworks, John Gillespie (ed.). Difficult-to-find études, toccatas, polkas, impromptus, waltzes, etc., by Albéniz, Bizet, Chabrier, Fauré, Smetana, Richard Strauss, Wagner and 16 other composers. 62 pieces. 343pp. 9 × 12. (Not available in France or Germany) 23447-9 Pa. **$15.95**

RARE MASTERPIECES OF RUSSIAN PIANO MUSIC: Eleven Pieces by Glinka, Balakirev, Glazunov and Others, edited by Dmitry Feofanov. Glinka's *Prayer,* Balakirev's *Reverie,* Liapunov's *Transcendental Etude, Op. 11, No. 10,* and eight others—full, authoritative scores from Russian texts. 144pp. 9 × 12. 24659-0 Pa. **$8.95**

NINETEENTH-CENTURY AMERICAN PIANO MUSIC, edited by John Gillespie. 40 pieces by 27 American composers: Gottschalk, Victor Herbert, Edward MacDowell, William Mason, Ethelbert Nevin, others. 323pp. 9 × 12. 23602-1 Pa. **$14.95**

PIANO MUSIC, Louis M. Gottschalk. 26 pieces (including covers) by early 19th-century American genius. "Bamboula," "The Banjo," other Creole, Negro-based material, through elegant salon music. 301pp. 9¼ × 12. 21683-7 Pa. **$12.95**

SOUSA'S GREAT MARCHES IN PIANO TRANSCRIPTION, John Philip Sousa. Playing edition includes: "The Stars and Stripes Forever," "King Cotton," "Washington Post," much more. 24 illustrations. 111pp. 9 × 12. 23132-1 Pa. **$6.95**

COMPLETE PIANO RAGS, Scott Joplin. All 38 piano rags by the acknowledged master of the form, reprinted from the publisher's original editions complete with sheet music covers. Introduction by David A. Jasen. 208pp. 9 × 12. 25807-6 Pa. **$9.95**

RAGTIME REDISCOVERIES, selected by Trebor Jay Tichenor. 64 unusual rags demonstrate diversity of style, local tradition. Original sheet music. 320pp. 9 × 12. 23776-1 Pa. **$11.95**

RAGTIME RARITIES, edited by Trebor J. Tichenor. 63 tuneful, rediscovered piano rags by 51 composers (or teams). Does not duplicate selections in *Classic Piano Rags* (Dover, 20469-3). 305pp. 9 × 12. 23157-7 Pa. **$12.95**

CLASSIC PIANO RAGS, selected with an introduction by Rudi Blesh. Best ragtime music (1897–1922) by Scott Joplin, James Scott, Joseph F. Lamb, Tom Turpin, nine others. 364pp. 9 × 12. 20469-3 Pa. **$14.95**

RAGTIME GEMS: Original Sheet Music for 25 Ragtime Classics, edited by David A. Jasen. Includes original sheet music and covers for 25 rags, including three of Scott Joplin's finest: *Searchlight Rag, Rose Leaf Rag* and *Fig Leaf Rag.* 122pp. 9 × 12. 25248-5 Pa. **$7.95**

NOCTURNES AND BARCAROLLES FOR SOLO PIANO, Gabriel Fauré. 12 nocturnes and 12 barcarolles reprinted from authoritative French editions. 208pp. 9⅜ × 12¼. (Not available in France or Germany) 27955-3 Pa. **$10.95**

PRELUDES AND FUGUES FOR PIANO, Dmitry Shostakovich. 24 Preludes, Op. 34 and 24 Preludes and Fugues, Op. 87. Reprint of Gosudarstvennoe Izdatel'stvo Muzyka, Moscow, ed. 288pp. 8⅜ × 11. (Available in U.S. only) 26861-6 Pa. **$12.95**

FAVORITE WALTZES, POLKAS AND OTHER DANCES FOR SOLO PIANO, Johann Strauss, Jr. Blue Danube, Tales from Vienna Woods, many other best-known waltzes and other dances. 160pp. 9 × 12. 27851-4 Pa. **$9.95**

SELECTED PIANO WORKS FOR FOUR HANDS, Franz Schubert. 24 separate pieces (16 most popular titles): Three Military Marches, Lebensstürme, Four Polonaises, Four Ländler, etc. Rehearsal numbers added. 273pp. 9 × 12. 23529-7 Pa. **$11.95**

*Available from your music dealer or write for **free** Music Catalog to Dover Publications, Inc., Dept. MUBI, 31 East 2nd Street, Mineola, N.Y. 11501.*

Dover Piano and Keyboard Editions

SHORTER WORKS FOR PIANOFORTE SOLO, Franz Schubert. All piano music except Sonatas, Dances, and a few unfinished pieces. Contains Wanderer, Impromptus, Moments Musicals, Variations, Scherzi, etc. Breitkopf and Härtel edition. 199pp. 9⅜ × 12¼. 22648-4 Pa. **$10.95**

WALTZES AND SCHERZOS, Frédéric Chopin. All of the Scherzos and nearly all (20) of the Waltzes from the authoritative Paderewski edition. Editorial commentary. 214pp. 9 × 12. (Available in U.S. only) 24316-8 Pa. **$9.95**

COMPLETE PRELUDES AND ETUDES FOR SOLO PIANO, Frédéric Chopin. All 26 Preludes, all 27 Etudes by greatest composer of piano music. Authoritative Paderewski edition. 224pp. 9 × 12. (Available in U.S. only) 24052-5 Pa. **$8.95**

COMPLETE BALLADES, IMPROMPTUS AND SONATAS, Frédéric Chopin. The four Ballades, four Impromptus and three Sonatas. Authoritative Paderewski edition. 240pp. 9 × 12. (Available in U.S. only) 24164-5 Pa. **$9.95**

NOCTURNES AND POLONAISES, Frédéric Chopin. 19 *Nocturnes* and 16 *Polonaises* reproduced from the authoritative Paderewski Edition for pianists, students, and musicologists. Commentary. viii + 272pp. 9 × 12. (Available in U.S. only) 24564-0 Pa. **$10.95**

COMPLETE MAZURKAS, Frédéric Chopin. 51 best-loved compositions, reproduced directly from the authoritative Kistner edition edited by Carl Mikuli. 160pp. 9 × 12. 25548-4 Pa. **$8.95**

FANTASY IN F MINOR, BARCAROLLE, BERCEUSE AND OTHER WORKS FOR SOLO PIANO, Frédéric Chopin. 15 works, including one of the greatest of the Romantic period, the Fantasy in F Minor, Op. 49, reprinted from the authoritative German edition prepared by Chopin's student, Carl Mikuli. 224pp. 8¾ × 11¼. 25950-1 Pa. **$7.95**

COMPLETE HUNGARIAN RHAPSODIES FOR SOLO PIANO, Franz Liszt. All 19 Rhapsodies reproduced directly from an authoritative Russian edition. All headings, footnotes translated to English. Best one volume edition available. 224pp. 8⅜ × 11¼. 24744-9 Pa. **$9.95**

ANNÉES DE PÈLERINAGE, COMPLETE, Franz Liszt. Authoritative Russian edition of piano masterpieces: *Première Année (Suisse): Deuxième Année (Italie)* and *Venezia e Napoli; Troisième Année*, other related pieces. 288pp. 9⅜ × 12¼. 25627-8 Pa. **$12.95**

COMPLETE ETUDES FOR SOLO PIANO, Series I: Including the Transcendental Etudes, Franz Liszt, edited by Busoni. Also includes Etude in 12 Exercises, 12 Grandes Etudes and Mazeppa. Breitkopf & Härtel edition. 272pp. 8⅜ × 11¼. 25815-7 Pa. **$11.95**

COMPLETE ETUDES FOR SOLO PIANO, Series II: Including the Paganini Etudes and Concert Etudes, Franz Liszt, edited by Busoni. Also includes Morceau de Salon, Ab Irato. Breitkopf & Härtel edition. 192pp. 8⅜ × 11¼. 25816-5 Pa. **$9.95**

SONATA IN B MINOR AND OTHER WORKS FOR PIANO, Franz Liszt. One of Liszt's most performed piano masterpieces, with the six Consolations, ten *Harmonies poetiques et religieuses*, two Ballades and two Legendes. Breitkopf and Härtel edition. 208pp. 8⅜ × 11¼. 26182-4 Pa. **$9.95**

PIANO TRANSCRIPTIONS FROM FRENCH AND ITALIAN OPERAS, Franz Liszt. Virtuoso transformations of themes by Mozart, Verdi, Bellini, other masters, into unforgettable music for piano. Published in association with American Liszt Society. 247pp. 9 × 12. 24273-0 Pa. **$12.95**

MEPHISTO WALTZ AND OTHER WORKS FOR SOLO PIANO, Franz Liszt. Rapsodie Espagnole, Liebestraüme Nos. 1–3, Valse Oubliée No. 1, Nuages Gris, Polonaises Nos. 1 and 2, Grand Galop Chromatique, more. 192pp. 8⅜ × 11¼. 28147-7 Pa. **$9.95**

COMPLETE WORKS FOR PIANOFORTE SOLO, Felix Mendelssohn. Breitkopf and Härtel edition of Capriccio in F# Minor, Sonata in E Major, Fantasy in F# Minor, Three Caprices, Songs without Words, and 20 other works. Total of 416pp. 9⅜ × 12¼. Two-vol. set. 23136-4, 23137-2 Pa. **$21.90**

COMPLETE SONATAS AND VARIATIONS FOR SOLO PIANO, Johannes Brahms. All sonatas, five variations on themes from Schumann, Paganini, Handel, etc. Vienna Gesellschaft der Musikfreunde edition. 178pp. 9 × 12. 22650-6 Pa. **$9.95**

COMPLETE SHORTER WORKS FOR SOLO PIANO, Johannes Brahms. All solo music not in other two volumes. Waltzes, Scherzo in E Flat Minor, Eight Pieces, Rhapsodies, Fantasies, Intermezzi, etc. Vienna Gesellschaft der Musikfreunde. 180pp. 9 × 12. 22651-4 Pa. **$9.95**

COMPLETE TRANSCRIPTIONS, CADENZAS AND EXERCISES FOR SOLO PIANO, Johannes Brahms. Vienna Gesellschaft der Musikfreunde edition, vol. 15. Studies after Chopin, Weber, Bach; gigues, sarabandes; 10 Hungarian dances, etc. 178pp. 9 × 12. 22652-2 Pa. **$9.95**

PIANO MUSIC OF ROBERT SCHUMANN, Series I, edited by Clara Schumann. Major compositions from the period 1830–39; *Papillons*, Toccata, Grosse Sonate No. 1, *Phantasiestücke, Arabeske, Blumenstück*, and nine other works. Reprinted from Breitkopf & Härtel edition. 274pp. 9⅜ × 12¼. 21459-1 Pa. **$12.95**

PIANO MUSIC OF ROBERT SCHUMANN, Series II, edited by Clara Schumann. Major compositions from period 1838–53; *Humoreske, Novelletten*, Sonate No. 2, 43 *Clavierstücke für die Jugend*, and six other works. Reprinted from Breitkopf & Härtel edition. 272pp. 9⅜ × 12¼. 21461-3 Pa. **$12.95**

PIANO MUSIC OF ROBERT SCHUMANN, Series III, edited by Clara Schumann. All solo music not in other two volumes, including *Symphonic Etudes, Phantaisie*, 13 other choice works. Definitive Breitkopf & Härtel edition. 224pp. 9⅜ × 12¼. 23906-3 Pa. $10.95

PIANO MUSIC 1888–1905, Claude Debussy. Deux Arabesques, Suite Bergamesque, Masques, first series of Images, etc. Nine others, in corrected editions. 175pp. 9⅜ × 12¼. 22771-5 Pa. **$7.95**

COMPLETE PRELUDES, Books 1 and 2, Claude Debussy. 24 evocative works that reveal the essence of Debussy's genius for musical imagery, among them many of the composer's most famous piano compositions. Glossary of French terms. 128pp. 8⅜ × 11¼. 25970-6 Pa. **$6.95**

PRELUDES, BOOK 1: The Autograph Score, Claude Debussy. Superb facsimile reproduced directly from priceless autograph score in Pierpont Morgan Library in New York. New Introduction by Roy Howat. 48pp. 8⅛ × 11. 25549-2 Pa. **$8.95**

PIANO MASTERPIECES OF MAURICE RAVEL, Maurice Ravel. Handsome affordable treasury; *Pavane pour une infante defunte, jeux d'eau, Sonatine, Miroirs*, more. 128pp. 9 × 12. (Not available in France or Germany) 25137-3 Pa. **$7.95**

COMPLETE LYRIC PIECES FOR PIANO, Edvard Grieg. All 66 pieces from Grieg's ten sets of little mood pictures for piano, favorites of generations of pianists. 224pp. 9⅜ × 12¼. 26176-X Pa. **$10.95**

Available from your music dealer or write for **free** *Music Catalog to*
Dover Publications, Inc., Dept. MUBI, 31 East 2nd Street, Mineola, N.Y. 11501.

Dover Orchestral Scores

THE SIX BRANDENBURG CONCERTOS AND THE FOUR ORCHESTRAL SUITES IN FULL SCORE, Johann Sebastian Bach. Complete standard Bach-Gesellschaft editions in large, clear format. Study score. 273pp. 9 × 12. 23376-6 Pa. **$10.95**

COMPLETE CONCERTI FOR SOLO KEYBOARD AND ORCHESTRA IN FULL SCORE, Johann Sebastian Bach. Bach's seven complete concerti for solo keyboard and orchestra in full score from the authoritative Bach-Gesellschaft edition. 206pp. 9 × 12. 24929-8 Pa. **$10.95**

THE THREE VIOLIN CONCERTI IN FULL SCORE, Johann Sebastian Bach. Concerto in A Minor, BWV 1041; Concerto in E Major, BWV 1042; and Concerto for Two Violins in D Minor, BWV 1043. Bach-Gesellschaft edition. 64pp. 9⅜ × 12¼. 25124-1 Pa. **$5.95**

GREAT ORGAN CONCERTI, OPP. 4 & 7, IN FULL SCORE, George Frideric Handel. 12 organ concerti composed by great Baroque master are reproduced in full score from the *Deutsche Handelgesellschaft* edition. 138pp. 9⅜ × 12¼. 24462-8 Pa. **$8.95**

COMPLETE CONCERTI GROSSI IN FULL SCORE, George Frideric Handel. Monumental Opus 6 Concerti Grossi, Opus 3 and "Alexander's Feast" Concerti Grossi—19 in all—reproduced from most authoritative edition. 258pp. 9⅜ × 12¼. 24187-4 Pa. **$12.95**

COMPLETE CONCERTI GROSSI IN FULL SCORE, Arcangelo Corelli. All 12 concerti in the famous late nineteenth-century edition prepared by violinist Joseph Joachim and musicologist Friedrich Chrysander. 240pp. 8⅜ × 11¼. 25606-5 Pa. **$12.95**

WATER MUSIC AND MUSIC FOR THE ROYAL FIREWORKS IN FULL SCORE, George Frideric Handel. Full scores of two of the most popular Baroque orchestral works performed today—reprinted from definitive Deutsche Handelgesellschaft edition. Total of 96pp. 8¼ × 11. 25070-9 Pa. **$6.95**

LATER SYMPHONIES, Wolfgang A. Mozart. Full orchestral scores to last symphonies (Nos. 35–41) reproduced from definitive Breitkopf & Härtel Complete Works edition. Study score. 285pp. 9 × 12. 23052-X Pa. **$11.95**

17 DIVERTIMENTI FOR VARIOUS INSTRUMENTS, Wolfgang A. Mozart. Sparkling pieces of great vitality and brilliance from 1771–1779; consecutively numbered from 1 to 17. Reproduced from definitive Breitkopf & Härtel Complete Works edition. Study score. 241pp. 9⅜ × 12¼. 23862-8 Pa. **$11.95**

PIANO CONCERTOS NOS. 11–16 IN FULL SCORE, Wolfgang Amadeus Mozart. Authoritative Breitkopf & Härtel edition of six staples of the concerto repertoire, including Mozart's cadenzas for Nos. 12–16. 256pp. 9⅜ × 12¼. 25468-2 Pa. **$12.95**

PIANO CONCERTOS NOS. 17–22, Wolfgang Amadeus Mozart. Six complete piano concertos in full score, with Mozart's own cadenzas for Nos. 17–19. Breitkopf & Härtel edition. Study score. 370pp. 9⅜ × 12¼. 23599-8 Pa. **$14.95**

PIANO CONCERTOS NOS. 23–27, Wolfgang Amadeus Mozart. Mozart's last five piano concertos in full score, plus cadenzas for Nos. 23 and 27, and the Concert Rondo in D Major, K.382. Breitkopf & Härtel edition. Study score. 310pp. 9⅜ × 12¼. 23600-5 Pa. **$12.95**

CONCERTI FOR WIND INSTRUMENTS IN FULL SCORE, Wolfgang Amadeus Mozart. Exceptional volume contains ten pieces for orchestra and wind instruments and includes some of Mozart's finest, most popular music. 272pp. 9⅜ × 12¼. 25228-0 Pa. **$12.95**

THE VIOLIN CONCERTI AND THE SINFONIA CONCERTANTE, K.364, IN FULL SCORE, Wolfgang Amadeus Mozart. All five violin concerti and famed double concerto reproduced from authoritative Breitkopf & Härtel Complete Works Edition. 208pp. 9⅜ × 12½. 25169-1 Pa. **$11.95**

SYMPHONIES 88–92 IN FULL SCORE: The Haydn Society Edition, Joseph Haydn. Full score of symphonies Nos. 88 through 92. Large, readable noteheads, ample margins for fingerings, etc., and extensive Editor's Commentary. 304pp. 9 × 12. (Available in U.S. only) 24445-8 Pa. **$13.95**

COMPLETE LONDON SYMPHONIES IN FULL SCORE, Series I and Series II, Joseph Haydn. Reproduced from the Eulenburg editions are Symphonies Nos. 93–98 (Series I) and Nos. 99–104 (Series II). 800pp. 8⅜ × 11¼. (Available in U.S. only) Series I 24982-4 Pa. **$15.95**
Series II 24983-2 Pa. **$16.95**

FOUR SYMPHONIES IN FULL SCORE, Franz Schubert. Schubert's four most popular symphonies: No. 4 in C Minor ("Tragic"); No. 5 in B-flat Major; No. 8 in B Minor ("Unfinished"); and No. 9 in C Major ("Great"). Breitkopf & Härtel edition. Study score. 261pp. 9⅜ × 12¼. 23681-1 Pa. **$11.95**

GREAT OVERTURES IN FULL SCORE, Carl Maria von Weber. Overtures to *Oberon, Der Freischutz, Euryanthe* and *Preciosa* reprinted from auhoritative Breitkopf & Härtel editions. 112pp. 9 × 12. 25225-6 Pa. **$8.95**

SYMPHONIES NOS. 1, 2, 3, AND 4 IN FULL SCORE, Ludwig van Beethoven. Republication of H. Litolff edition. 272pp. 9 × 12. 26033-X Pa. **$10.95**

SYMPHONIES NOS. 5, 6 AND 7 IN FULL SCORE, Ludwig van Beethoven. Republication of the H. Litolff edition. 272pp. 9 × 12. 26034-8 Pa. **$10.95**

SYMPHONIES NOS. 8 AND 9 IN FULL SCORE, Ludwig van Beethoven. Republication of the H. Litolff edition. 256pp. 9 × 12. 26035-6 Pa. **$10.95**

SIX GREAT OVERTURES IN FULL SCORE, Ludwig van Beethoven. Six staples of the orchestral repertoire from authoritative Breitkopf & Härtel edition. *Leonore Overtures,* Nos. 1–3; Overtures to *Coriolanus, Egmont, Fidelio.* 288pp. 9 × 12. 24789-9 Pa. **$12.95**

COMPLETE PIANO CONCERTOS IN FULL SCORE, Ludwig van Beethoven. Complete scores of five great Beethoven piano concertos, with all cadenzas as he wrote them, reproduced from authoritative Breitkopf & Härtel edition. New table of contents. 384pp. 9⅜ × 12¼. 24563-2 Pa. **$14.95**

GREAT ROMANTIC VIOLIN CONCERTI IN FULL SCORE, Ludwig van Beethoven, Felix Mendelssohn and Peter Ilyitch Tchaikovsky. The Beethoven Op. 61, Mendelssohn, Op. 64 and Tchaikovsky, Op. 35 concertos reprinted from the Breitkopf & Härtel editions. 224pp. 9 × 12. 24989-1 Pa. **$10.95**

MAJOR ORCHESTRAL WORKS IN FULL SCORE, Felix Mendelssohn. Generally considered to be Mendelssohn's finest orchestral works, here in one volume are: the complete *Midsummer Night's Dream; Hebrides Overture; Calm Sea and Prosperous Voyage Overture;* Symphony No. 3 in A ("Scottish"); and Symphony No. 4 in A ("Italian"). Breitkopf & Härtel edition. Study score. 406pp. 9 × 12. 23184-4 Pa. **$16.95**

COMPLETE SYMPHONIES, Johannes Brahms. Full orchestral scores. No. 1 in C Minor, Op. 68; No. 2 in D Major, Op. 73; No. 3 in F Major, Op. 90; and No. 4 in E Minor, Op. 98. Reproduced from definitive Vienna Gesellschaft der Musikfreunde edition. Study score. 344pp. 9 × 12. 23053-8 Pa. **$13.95**

Available from your music dealer or write for free Music Catalog to
Dover Publications, Inc., Dept. MUBI, 31 East 2nd Street, Mineola, N.Y. 11501.

Dover Orchestral Scores

THREE ORCHESTRAL WORKS IN FULL SCORE: Academic Festival Overture, Tragic Overture and Variations on a Theme by Joseph Haydn, Johannes Brahms. Reproduced from the authoritative Breitkopf & Härtel edition three of Brahms's great orchestral favorites. Editor's commentary in German and English. 112pp. 9⅜ × 12¼.
24637-X Pa. **$8.95**

COMPLETE CONCERTI IN FULL SCORE, Johannes Brahms. Piano Concertos Nos. 1 and 2; Violin Concerto, Op. 77; Concerto for Violin and Cello, Op. 102. Definitive Breitkopf & Härtel edition. 352pp. 9⅜ × 12¼.
24170-X Pa. **$14.95**

COMPLETE SYMPHONIES IN FULL SCORE, Robert Schumann. No. 1 in B-flat Major, Op. 38 ("Spring"); No. 2 in C Major, Op. 61; No. 3 in E Flat Major, Op. 97 ("Rhenish"); and No. 4 in D Minor, Op. 120. Breitkopf & Härtel editions. Study score. 416pp. 9⅜ × 12¼.
24013-4 Pa. **$17.95**

GREAT WORKS FOR PIANO AND ORCHESTRA IN FULL SCORE, Robert Schumann. Collection of three superb pieces for piano and orchestra, including the popular Piano Concerto in A Minor. Breitkopf & Härtel edition. 183pp. 9⅜ × 12¼.
24340-0 Pa. **$9.95**

THE PIANO CONCERTOS IN FULL SCORE, Frédéric Chopin. The authoritative Breitkopf & Härtel full-score edition in one volume of Piano Concertos No. 1 in E Minor and No. 2 in F Minor. 176pp. 9 × 12.
25835-1 Pa. **$9.95**

THE PIANO CONCERTI IN FULL SCORE, Franz Liszt. Available in one volume the Piano Concerto No. 1 in E-flat Major and the Piano Concerto No. 2 in A Major—are among the most studied, recorded and performed of all works for piano and orchestra. 144pp. 9 × 12.
25221-3 Pa. **$8.95**

SYMPHONY NO. 8 IN G MAJOR, OP. 88, SYMPHONY NO. 9 IN E MINOR, OP. 95 ("NEW WORLD") IN FULL SCORE, Antonín Dvořák. Two celebrated symphonies by the great Czech composer, the Eighth and the immensely popular Ninth, "From the New World" in one volume. 272pp. 9 × 12.
24749-X Pa. **$12.95**

FOUR ORCHESTRAL WORKS IN FULL SCORE: Rapsodie Espagnole, Mother Goose Suite, Valses Nobles et Sentimentales, and Pavane for a Dead Princess, Maurice Ravel. Four of Ravel's most popular orchestral works, reprinted from original full-score French editions. 240pp. 9⅜ × 12¼. (Not available in France or Germany)
25962-5 Pa. **$11.95**

DAPHNIS AND CHLOE IN FULL SCORE, Maurice Ravel. Definitive full-score edition of Ravel's rich musical setting of a Greek fable by Longus is reprinted here from the original French edition. 320pp. 9⅜ × 12¼. (Not available in France or Germany) 25826-2 Pa. **$14.95**

THREE GREAT ORCHESTRAL WORKS IN FULL SCORE, Claude Debussy. Three favorites by influential modernist: *Prélude à l'Après-midi d'un Faune, Nocturnes,* and *La Mer.* Reprinted from early French editions. 279pp. 9 × 12.
24441-5 Pa. **$12.95**

SYMPHONY IN D MINOR IN FULL SCORE, César Franck. Superb, authoritative edition of Franck's only symphony, an often-performed and recorded masterwork of late French romantic style. 160pp. 9 × 12.
25373-2 Pa. **$9.95**

THE GREAT WALTZES IN FULL SCORE, Johann Strauss, Jr. Complete scores of eight melodic masterpieces: The Beautiful Blue Danube, Emperor Waltz, Tales of the Vienna Woods, Wiener Blut, four more. Authoritative editions. 336pp. 8⅜ × 11¼. 26009-7 Pa. **$13.95**

FOURTH, FIFTH AND SIXTH SYMPHONIES IN FULL SCORE, Peter Ilyitch Tchaikovsky. Complete orchestral scores of Symphony No. 4 in F minor, Op. 36; Symphony No. 5 in E minor, Op. 64; Symphony No. 6 in B minor, "Pathetique," Op. 74. Study score. Breitkopf & Härtel editions. 480pp. 9⅜ × 12¼. 23861-X Pa. **$19.95**

ROMEO AND JULIET OVERTURE AND CAPRICCIO ITALIEN IN FULL SCORE, Peter Ilyitch Tchaikovsky. Two of Russian master's most popular compositions in high quality, inexpensive reproduction. From authoritative Russian edition. 208pp. 8⅜ × 11½.
25217-5 Pa. **$9.95**

NUTCRACKER SUITE IN FULL SCORE, Peter Ilyitch Tchaikovsky. Among the most popular ballet pieces ever created—a complete, inexpensive, high-quality score to study and enjoy. 128pp. 9 × 12.
25379-1 Pa. **$7.95**

TONE POEMS, SERIES I: DON JUAN, TOD UND VERKLARUNG, and DON QUIXOTE, Richard Strauss. Three of the most often performed and recorded works in entire orchestral repertoire, reproduced in full score from original editions. Study score. 286pp. 9⅜ × 12¼. (Available in U.S. only) 23754-0 Pa. **$13.95**

TONE POEMS, SERIES II: TILL EULENSPIEGELS LUSTIGE STREICHE, ALSO SPRACH ZARATHUSTRA, and EIN HELDENLEBEN, Richard Strauss. Three important orchestral works, including very popular *Till Eulenspiegel's Merry Pranks,* reproduced in full score from original editions. Study score. 315pp. 9⅜ × 12¼. (Available in U.S. only) 23755-9 Pa. **$14.95**

DAS LIED VON DER ERDE IN FULL SCORE, Gustav Mahler. Mahler's masterpiece, a fusion of song and symphony, reprinted from the original 1912 Universal Edition. English translations of song texts. 160pp. 9 × 12. 25657-X Pa. **$8.95**

SYMPHONIES NOS. 1 AND 2 IN FULL SCORE, Gustav Mahler. Unabridged, authoritative Austrian editions of Symphony No. 1 in D Major ("Titan") and Symphony No. 2 in C Minor ("Resurrection"). 384pp. 8⅜ × 11. 25473-9 Pa. **$14.95**

SYMPHONIES NOS. 3 AND 4 IN FULL SCORE, Gustav Mahler. Two brilliantly contrasting masterworks—one scored for a massive ensemble, the other for small orchestra and soloist—reprinted from authoritative Viennese editions. 368pp. 9⅜ × 12¼. 26166-2 Pa. **$15.95**

SYMPHONY NO. 8 IN FULL SCORE, Gustav Mahler. Superb authoritative edition of massive, complex "Symphony of a Thousand." Scored for orchestra, eight solo voices, double chorus, boys' choir and organ. Reprint of Izdatel'stvo "Muzyka," Moscow, edition. Translation of texts. 272pp. 9⅜ × 12¼. 26022-4 Pa. **$12.95**

THE FIREBIRD IN FULL SCORE (Original 1910 Version), Igor Stravinsky. Handsome, inexpensive edition of modern masterpiece, renowned for brilliant orchestration, glowing color. Authoritative Russian edition. 176pp. 9⅜ × 12¼. (Available in U.S. only)
25535-2 Pa. **$9.95**

PETRUSHKA IN FULL SCORE: Original Version, Igor Stravinsky. The definitive full-score edition of Stravinsky's masterful score for the great Ballets Russes 1911 production of *Petrushka.* 160pp. 9⅜ × 12¼. (Available in U.S. only) 25680-4 Pa. **$9.95**

THE RITE OF SPRING IN FULL SCORE, Igor Stravinsky. A reprint of the original full-score edition of the most famous musical work of the 20th century, created as a ballet score for Diaghilev's Ballets Russes. 176pp. 9⅜ × 12¼. (Available in U.S. only) 25857-2 Pa. **$9.95**

Available from your music dealer or write for ***free*** *Music Catalog to Dover Publications, Inc., Dept. MUBI, 31 East 2nd Street, Mineola, N.Y. 11501.*

Dover Chamber Music Scores

COMPLETE SUITES FOR UNACCOMPANIED CELLO AND SONATAS FOR VIOLA DA GAMBA, Johann Sebastian Bach. Bach-Gesellschaft edition of the six cello suites (BWV 1007–1012) and three sonatas (BWV 1027–1029), commonly played today on the cello. 112pp. 9⅜ × 12¼. 25641-3 Pa. **$8.95**

WORKS FOR VIOLIN, Johann Sebastian Bach. Complete Sonatas and Partitas for Unaccompanied Violin; Six Sonatas for Violin and Clavier. Bach-Gesellschaft edition. 158pp. 9⅜ × 12¼. 23683-8 Pa. **$8.95**

COMPLETE STRING QUARTETS, Wolfgang A. Mozart. Breitkopf & Härtel edition. All 23 string quartets plus alternate slow movement to K.156. Study score. 277pp. 9⅜ × 12¼. 22372-8 Pa. **$12.95**

COMPLETE STRING QUINTETS, Wolfgang Amadeus Mozart. All the standard-instrumentation string quintets, plus String Quintet in C Minor, K.406; Quintet with Horn or Second Cello, K.407; and Clarinet Quintet, K.581. Breitkopf & Härtel edition. Study score. 181pp. 9⅜ × 12¼. 23603-X Pa. **$8.95**

STRING QUARTETS, OPP. 20 and 33, COMPLETE, Joseph Haydn. Complete reproductions of the 12 masterful quartets (six each) of Opp. 20 and 33—in the reliable Eulenburg edition. 272pp. 8⅜ × 11¼. 24852-6 Pa. **$12.95**

STRING QUARTETS, OPP. 42, 50 and 54, Joseph Haydn. Complete reproductions of Op. 42 in D minor; Op. 50, Nos. 1–6 ("Prussian Quartets") and Op. 54, Nos. 1–3. Reliable Eulenburg edition. 224pp. 8⅜ × 11¼. 24262-5 Pa. **$11.95**

TWELVE STRING QUARTETS, Joseph Haydn. 12 often-performed works: Op. 55, Nos. 1–3 (including *Razor*); Op. 64, Nos. 1–6; Op. 71, Nos. 1–3. Definitive Eulenburg edition. 288pp. 8⅜ × 11¼. 23933-0 Pa. **$11.95**

ELEVEN LATE STRING QUARTETS, Joseph Haydn. Complete reproductions of Op. 74, Nos. 1–3; Op. 76, Nos. 1–6; and Op. 77, Nos. 1 and 2. Definitive Eulenburg edition. Full-size study score. 320pp. 8⅜ × 11¼. 23753-2 Pa. **$12.95**

COMPLETE STRING QUARTETS, Ludwig van Beethoven. Breitkopf & Härtel edition. Six quartets of Opus 18; three quartets of Opus 59; Opera 74, 95, 127, 130, 131, 132, 135 and Grosse Fuge. Study score. 434pp. 9⅜ × 12¼. 22361-2 Pa. **$15.95**

SIX GREAT PIANO TRIOS IN FULL SCORE, Ludwig van Beethoven. Definitive Breitkopf & Härtel edition of Beethoven's Piano Trios Nos. 1–6 including the "Ghost" and the "Archduke". 224pp. 9⅜ × 12¼. 25398-8 Pa. **$10.95**

COMPLETE VIOLIN SONATAS, Ludwig van Beethoven. All ten sonatas including the "Kreutzer" and "Spring" sonatas in the definitive Breitkopf & Härtel edition. 256pp. 9 × 12. 26277-4 Pa. **$12.95**

COMPLETE SONATAS AND VARIATIONS FOR CELLO AND PIANO, Ludwig van Beethoven. All five sonatas and three sets of variations. Reprinted from Breitkopf & Härtel edition. 176pp. 9⅜ × 12¼. 26441-6 Pa. **$10.95**

COMPLETE CHAMBER MUSIC FOR STRINGS, Franz Schubert. Reproduced from famous Breitkopf & Härtel edition: Quintet in C Major (1828), 15 quartets and two trios for violin(s), viola, and violincello. Study score. 348pp. 9 × 12. 21463-X Pa. **$14.95**

COMPLETE CHAMBER MUSIC FOR PIANOFORTE AND STRINGS, Franz Schubert. Breitkopf & Härtel edition. *Trout*, Quartet in F Major, and trios for piano, violin, cello. Study score. 192pp. 9 × 12. 21527-X Pa. **$9.95**

CHAMBER WORKS FOR PIANO AND STRINGS, Felix Mendelssohn. Eleven of the composer's best known works in the genre—duos, trios, quartets and a sextet—reprinted from authoritative Breitkopf & Härtel edition. 384pp. 9⅜ × 12¼. 26117-4 Pa. **$15.95**

COMPLETE CHAMBER MUSIC FOR STRINGS, Felix Mendelssohn. All of Mendelssohn's chamber music: Octet, Two Quintets, Six Quartets, and Four Pieces for String Quartet. (Nothing with piano is included). Complete works edition (1874–7). Study score. 283pp. 9⅜ × 12¼. 23679-X Pa. **$12.95**

CHAMBER MUSIC OF ROBERT SCHUMANN, edited by Clara Schumann. Superb collection of three trios, four quartets, and piano quintet. Breitkopf & Härtel edition. 288pp. 9⅜ × 12¼. 24101-7 Pa. **$12.95**

COMPLETE SONATAS FOR SOLO INSTRUMENT AND PIANO, Johannes Brahms. All seven sonatas—three for violin, two for cello and two for clarinet (or viola)—reprinted from the authoritative Breitkopf & Härtel edition. 208pp. 9 × 12. 26091-7 Pa. **$11.95**

COMPLETE CHAMBER MUSIC FOR STRINGS AND CLARINET QUINTET, Johannes Brahms. Vienna Gesellschaft der Musikfreunde edition of all quartets, quintets, and sextet without piano. Study edition. 262pp. 8⅜ × 11¼. 21914-3 Pa. **$11.95**

QUINTET AND QUARTETS FOR PIANO AND STRINGS, Johannes Brahms. Full scores of *Quintet in F Minor*, Op. 34; *Quartet in G Minor*, Op. 25; *Quartet in A Major*, Op. 26; *Quartet in C Minor*, Op. 60. Breitkopf & Härtel edition. 298pp. 9 × 12. 24900-X Pa. **$13.95**

COMPLETE PIANO TRIOS, Johannes Brahms. All five piano trios in the definitive Breitkopf & Härtel edition. 288pp. 9 × 12. 25769-X Pa. **$13.95**

CHAMBER WORKS FOR PIANO AND STRINGS, Antonín Dvořák. Society editions of the F Minor and Dumky piano trios, D Major and E-flat Major piano quartets and A Major piano quintet. 352pp. 8⅜ × 11¼. (Available in U.S. only) 25663-4 Pa. **$15.95**

FIVE LATE STRING QUARTETS, Antonín Dvořák. Treasury of Czech master's finest chamber works: Nos. 10, 11, 12, 13, 14. Reliable Simrock editions. 282pp. 8⅜ × 11. 25135-7 Pa. **$11.95**

STRING QUARTETS BY DEBUSSY AND RAVEL/Claude Debussy: Quartet in G Minor, Op. 10/Maurice Ravel: Quartet in F Major, Claude Debussy and Maurice Ravel. Authoritative one-volume edition of two influential masterpieces noted for individuality, delicate and subtle beauties. 112pp. 8⅜ × 11. (Not available in France or Germany) 25231-0 Pa. **$7.95**

GREAT CHAMBER WORKS, César Franck. Four Great works: Violin Sonata in A Major, Piano Trio in F-sharp Minor, String Quartet in D Major and Piano Quintet in F Minor. From J. Hamelle, Paris and C. F. Peters, Leipzig editions. 248pp. 9⅜ × 12¼. **26546-3 Pa. $13.95**

DATE DUE